D0348523

TIME OUT

Gary E. Hurst, Mike Kachura,
and Larry D. Sides

*Daily Devotions
for Workaholics*

❖ *A Janet Thoma Book* ❖

THOMAS NELSON PUBLISHERS
Nashville

The Twelve Steps
1. We admitted we were powerless over alcohol—that our lives had become unmanageable. 2. Came to believe that a Power greater than ourselves could restore us to sanity. 3. Made a decision to turn our will and our lives over to the care of God, as we understood Him. 4. Made a searching and fearless moral inventory of ourselves. 5. Admitted to God, to ourselves, and to another human being the exact nature of our wrongs. 6. Were entirely ready to have God remove all these defects of character. 7. Humbly asked Him to remove our shortcomings. 8. Made a list of all persons we had harmed and became willing to make amends to them all. 9. Made direct amends to such people wherever possible, except when to do so would injure them or others. 10. Continued to take personal inventory and when we were wrong, promptly admitted it. 11. Sought through prayer and meditation to improve our conscious contact with God, praying only for knowledge of His will for us and the power to carry that out. 12. Having had a spiritual awakening as the result of these steps, we tried to carry this message to others, and to practice these principles in all our affairs.

❖ *A Janet Thoma Book* ❖

Copyright © 1991 by Gary E. Hurst, Mike Kachura, and Larry D. Sides

All rights reserved. Written permission must be secured from the publisher to use or reproduce any part of this book, except for brief quotations in critical reviews or articles.

Published in Nashville, Tennessee, by Thomas Nelson, Inc., and distributed in Canada by Lawson Falle, Ltd., Cambridge, Ontario.

Scripture quotations marked NAS are from THE NEW AMERICAN STANDARD BIBLE, Copyright © 1960, 1962, 1963, 1968, 1971, 1972, 1973, 1975, 1977 by The Lockman Foundation and are used by permission.

Scripture quotations are from the NEW KING JAMES VERSION of the Bible. Copyright © 1979, 1980, 1982, Thomas Nelson, Inc., Publishers.

Scripture quotations taken from The Holy Bible: NEW INTERNATIONAL VERSION are marked NIV. Copyright © 1978 by the New York International Bible Society. Used by permission of Zondervan Bible Publishers.

Library of Congress Cataloging-in-Publication Data

Hurst, Gary.
    Time out : daily devotions for workaholics / Gary Hurst, Mike Kachura, Larry Sides.
        p.   cm.— (Serenity meditation series)
    ISBN 0-8407-3342-9
    1. Workaholics—Prayer-books and devotions—English. 2. Twelve-step programs—Meditations. 3. Devotional calendars. I. Kachura, Mike. II. Sides, Larry. III. Title. IV. Series.
BV4596.W67H87 1991
242'.2—dc20   91-24302
                                                                            CIP

Printed in the United States of America
1 2 3 4 5 6 7 — 96 95 94 93 92 91

The Twelve Steps

1. We admitted we were powerless over work—that our lives had become unmanageable.
2. Came to believe that a Power greater than ourselves could restore us to sanity.
3. Made a decision to turn our will and our lives over to the care of God, as we understood Him.
4. Made a searching and fearless moral inventory of ourselves.
5. Admitted to God, to ourselves, and to another human being the exact nature of our wrongs.
6. Were entirely ready to have God remove all these defects of character.
7. Humbly asked Him to remove our shortcomings.
8. Made a list of all persons we had harmed and became willing to make amends to them all.
9. Made direct amends to such people wherever possible, except when to do so would injure them or others.
10. Continued to take personal inventory and when we were wrong, promptly admitted it.
11. Sought through prayer and meditation to improve our conscious contact with God, praying only for knowledge of His will for us and the power to carry that out.
12. Having had a spiritual awakening as the result of these steps, we tried to carry this message to others, and to practice these principles in all our affairs.

Introduction

In our more than thirty years of working with individuals and their families we have seen the devastation—sometimes camouflaged and sometimes not—of the effects of workaholism. The three of us have received countless phone calls and requests from clients. At times we should have said no but as men susceptible to the same weaknesses as other people, we did not.

On more than a few occasions while working on this devotional we have had to confess to one another that we were being workaholics in the process of attempting to minister to workaholics. Only our mutual accountability and constant attention to the principles about which we were writing kept us from drowning in our work.

The process of overcoming the tendency to work-as-though-your-life-depended-on-it is a journey called life that consists of countless, small choices. It is not a singular choice that creates a workaholic, but the accumulation of those. It is our hope and prayer that the regular application of these principles that have helped curb our own tendencies toward workaholism will help you to find healing and to build your own collection of healthy choices for a more satisfying journey through life.

God bless you,

Gary, Mike, & Larry

NEW YEAR'S RESOLUTION – *January 1*

Commit your works to the LORD,
And your thoughts will be established.
—PROV. 16:3

You enter this New Year recognizing that you have a problem with how you work. You may have been to this crossroads before and made a resolution to work less. You may have promised yourself to spend more time with God, too.

I recommend that you not make a New Year's resolution about work. In order for any of your efforts to recover from a work addiction to be successful, you must begin by removing the pressure of an unrealistic goal.

As trite as it may sound, a one-day-at-a-time approach is probably more realistic. In using this devotional guide, for example, there may be days when you don't do it, days when you wish you never began, and days when you want to rush the recovery process.

Follow the suggestion of today's Bible verse and commit it to God. Talk to him and study his Word beyond what is in this devotional.

Father, I want to give you my strong attachment to my work. Be my constant companion as I begin this journey. I trust you to hold me up during those tough times.

> *Indeed we count them blessed who endure. You have heard of the perseverance of Job and seen the end intended by the Lord—that the Lord is very compassionate and merciful.* —JAMES 5:11

I recently read about a research project performed on monkeys. A monkey was strapped to a chair for six hours a day and received mild shocks at twenty-second intervals. The monkey could cancel the shock at any time by pushing a red button. After three weeks the monkey died of a perforated ulcer. The next time a companion monkey was set up next to the experimental monkey. This time the companion monkey also received shocks, whether it pushed the button or not. After the three weeks this companion monkey was happy and adjusted. The experimental monkey, again, died from a perforated ulcer. The scientists concluded that the stress of *decision making* overloaded the experimental monkey. The companion monkey adjusted to the pain; the experimental monkey died from trying to avoid it.

Perhaps this is a warning to you who are in leadership positions to control the stress; perhaps it is a note to those of us who are not in the decision-making seat to appreciate the stress on those who are.

Lord, help us endure the pain of life and not avoid it.

And you are complete in Him.
—COL. 2:10

We were camping at an African game park. Bob was married and I was single, but this particular night we were both "baching it." His wife was back in the States for her sister's wedding, and we had all predicted that Bob would fall apart without Ilene. They were so devoted to each other and worked so well as a team that this separation should have caused Bob to founder without her. So we thought.

But Bob was fine, and that intrigued me. So that night in the tent our conversation frequently touched on things like satisfaction, fulfillment, contentment, and the like. When asked directly how he was doing without Ilene around, Bob responded, "Well, when you are complete in Christ. . . ."

I can't recall how he finished his answer. My belief had been that people's personal successes, their "completeness," had to do with achievement, relationships, accomplishments, and power.

What makes you complete? It's worth an honest inventory.

> *[We] ask that you may be filled with the*
> *knowledge of His will in all wisdom and*
> *spiritual understanding; that you may have*
> *a walk worthy of the Lord, fully pleasing Him,*
> *being fruitful in every good work and increasing*
> *in the knowledge of God.* —COL. 1:9–10

The sweetest part of our recovery is our new relationship with Christ. With this comes a new purpose and calling that transcends our former nature. The circumstances of our life remain unchanged, but now we view them differently.

We desire to live a life that is pleasing to God yet with less anxiety about how well we are shaping up with God. Our chief end becomes to love him and serve him for the rest of our life.

God will complete a good work in you and will empower you to do his will. That is a blessed assurance, given the long journey you have traveled. Remember to always be like a child in your relationship to Christ. Stand back and watch his might convert you.

Lord, you are the greatest! Keep me close to you so I may know how to work for you.

I know that there is nothing better for them than to rejoice, and to do good in their lives.

—ECCL. 3:12

Abraham Lincoln once gave some insight on his work ethic. "My father taught me how to work, but not to love it," he said. "I never did like to work and I don't deny it. I'd rather read, tell stories, crack jokes, talk, laugh,—anything but work." Is this the consummate workaholic you'd think it would take to get to the White House? Is this the same person who walked twenty miles to borrow a book? Is this the same Lincoln who never gave up the fight? It would be easy to assume he was a driven person, but he was not. Yet he attained the office of president over others who were far more driven than he. Notice, I did not say, *ambitious;* no one can face defeat as often as Lincoln and still become president without being ambitious.

The moral is this: you may be fun loving and accomplish more in life than you believed. The reverse is true also: you can work incessantly and die insignificantly. Workaholics believe that the latter is the only acceptable way to live. They often find out at midlife that the driven life does not pay off. Let us learn from Lincoln— he kept that balance and turned out all right, don't you think?

Do not live to work—work to live.

> *I know how to be abased, and I know how to*
> *abound.*
> —PHIL. 4:12

My two-year-old son is already pretty good at count-ing. He can make it to twelve without a hitch, but from there on it's a real hodgepodge of numbers.

Personally, I can't remember when I mastered arithmetic. Probably by the time I was in second or third grade I could dazzle aunts and uncles with dis-plays of counting prowess. You know, things like, "I can count to a hundred faster than you can!" and "I know how many zeroes there are in the number google, do you?"

But now I've learned to be more sophisticated, so I focus more on *what* to count rather than just *how* to count. Now it is things like, "How much money did we spend this month?" and "How long since my family last did something nice for me?"

There is a subtle trap there, and it is one I almost always find when I am in "work gear" or "go gear" or "compulsive gear." It is the trap of counting what is lost more than what is left.

Where is your spiritual focus today? Does your attitude emphasize what you have lost and/or not attained? Or what you have left for which to be grateful?

O God, You know my foolishness;
And my sins are not hidden from You.
—PS. 69:5

Steve prided himself on his organizational ability. His co-workers envied his ability to stay on track and meet deadlines. He never realized, however, that his list-keeping went far beyond what a successful person needed to be competent. Steve had lists of his lists. He always had a list on his mind.

Steve's family was frustrated with his expectation that they be organized at home and follow the routines he had set up. Eventually his teenage children began to rebel. During family counseling, Steve presented the problem in a very organized way, bringing with him a list of all his children's failures. A few minutes later his teenage son blurted out, "I'm sick of you and your lists!"

After several months of counseling alone and with his family, Steve learned to loosen up and let go of his lists. At first this made him anxious, but soon he learned that sometimes you need to take time to re-ward yourself for a job well done.

Father, teach me to stop and rest and enjoy the fruits of the labor you give me.

> *"Therefore if you bring your gift to the altar, and
> there remember that your brother has something
> against you, leave your gift there before the altar,
> and go your way. First be reconciled to your
> brother, and then come and offer your gift."*
> —MATT. 5:23–24

We tend to live with the misbelief that what we do is
our business and is of no concern to anyone else. The
alcoholic who says, "It is my body," the workaholic
who justifies her overwork because the family is bene-
fiting financially from it, are examples of this illusion.
Nothing could be further from the truth. Most therapists agree that there is an unbreakable bond between
the actions of a family member and the rest of the family. That's why we must make amends for the injuries
we have caused others if we are going to experience
healing and recovery.

Another myth states that it is humiliating and de-
grading to admit you are wrong. The opposite is true:
A person is never more noble than when he admits he
is wrong and seeks restitution.

*The verse for today reflects a theme that is evident throughout Scrip-
ture: if you have offended someone it is your responsibility to seek
reconciliation. Make amends to someone you have harmed.*

"Therefore you shall be perfect, just as your Father in heaven is perfect."
—MATT. 5:48

Janie had to be one of the most forlorn-looking women I had ever seen. Only a few hairs were in place, her wardrobe was functional at best, and her tired eyes confirmed any doubts about the heavy load she was carrying. Tomorrow would be her son's day in court. Grand larceny. A tough charge for a pre-sixteen-year-old. And his guilt was not in question.

Janie knew the commandments. Since she was convinced that she had *not* fulfilled her duties, she knew God must be as disappointed with her as she was. After all, he demands perfection and she had proof of her failure as a parent.

Her assumption was that a "good" parent has "good," healthy, spiritual children. Janie had not done everything right, but she was trying to carry her children's responsibilities. Perfectionists and workaholics often do that.

Think about this: First, there are no perfect parents on earth. The word perfect *in Matthew 5 carries the idea of maturity. Second, there is one perfect parent: our heavenly Father. And even when he had sinless children (Adam and Eve) in a perfect environment (the garden), they messed up.*

The discretion of a man makes him slow to anger,
And it is to his glory to overlook a transgression.
—PROV. 19:11

Jeff said he felt like his anger was a bottomless pit. He was working hard at letting go of control, but he was discouraged that this seemed to result in so much anger. First, there was the anger at his family for their overly high expectations. Then there was the anger at his children for still needing things when he felt so needy himself. This was followed by anger at his wife for not being sensitive and understanding, and finally there was the anger at himself for all the years of self-deprivation for nothing. It was indeed hard to give up control. Each layer of anger was like peeling off the layers of an onion. It was not pleasant work for Jeff, who had always thought that talking about feelings was unproductive. But he was past denial now and there was no turning back.

This early phase of recovery is often the scariest, but there is hope. You will find peace and healing and a life where needs are met and relationships are whole.

Lord, please help me release my anger to you. Forgive all my futile attempts at trying to be in control.

A merry heart does good, like medicine,
But a broken spirit dries the bones.
—PROV. 17:22

Norman Cousins died in 1990. He lived almost twenty years longer than anyone expected. Cousins, an author and journalist, had been diagnosed with a debilitating disease in the seventies. Instead of giving in to depression and despair he aided his recovery by immersing himself in humor. He watched cartoons, Laurel and Hardy films, and read anything that would make him laugh. It worked. His recovery was much swifter than the doctors predicted.

What happens when we laugh? The brain releases chemicals called endorphins which give us our feelings of well-being. On the other hand, stress depletes vital neurochemicals, bringing on depression and anxiety. It is very important, therefore, to cultivate your sense of humor.

God presented this concept long before science was able to verify it. A merry heart necessitates that we allow ourselves the opportunity to relax and enjoy the fruits of our labors. We must be careful not to write off lightness as foolish and trivial. Do not be fooled into thinking that life is all serious business.

Oppression makes even a wise man mad.

> *So teach us to number our days,*
> *That we may gain a heart of wisdom.*
> —PS. 90:12

Every American has them. In fact, we could not get along without more than one of them. And we seem to have them everywhere:

- The kitchen has at least one, usually two or three.
- For some time now they have been standard equipment in our automobiles.
- Every place of business has at least one.
- We even have them built into our personal computers.
- We wear them on our wrists.

You probably guessed it: watches, clocks, and other timepieces. Can you even count how many you use in a normal day? The workaholic tends to value minutes and hours as some of the most valuable of all resources.

But living in Africa for two years jolted this part of my Americanism. You see, Africans do not have clocks, but calendars. They count days, not minutes. They live longer, too. Is that a coincidence?

The Scripture talks about counting days and we talk about the one-minute manager. The African culture is present-day proof of which method works better in the long run.

But if we walk in the light as He is in the light, we have fellowship with one another.

—1 JOHN 1:7

One of the challenges of living in a large city like Washington, D.C., is developing meaningful relationships with others. So much energy must be put into survival-oriented pursuits that leisure must be crammed in. When we first arrived in the area we knew we needed to establish our own community network, so we invited others we had met over for dinner on a weekend. Most of those we invited came and were thrilled to have this opportunity. However, as time went on we were becoming fatigued because there was very little reciprocity.

What we have learned three years later is that at the end of a busy week people often don't feel like socializing. Socializing seems to be seen as another production, and consequently people avoid it. Unfortunately, this can lead to a sense of alienation and absence of community. If we are going to build toward a better tomorrow we must not lose the importance of community.

_____

Lord, I am weary from my labors. Help me to form healthy bonds with others in spite of my fatigue.

> *But he himself went a day's journey into the*
> *wilderness, and came and sat down under a broom*
> *tree. And he prayed that he might die, and said, "It*
> *is enough! Now, LORD, take my life."*
> —1 KINGS 19:4

A scene from the Jimmy Stewart movie *The Spirit of St. Louis* stands out in my mind. Stewart portrays Charles Lindbergh during his historical flight across the Atlantic. The greatest battle that he fought was the desire to fall asleep. Watching Stewart made me feel the same excruciating fatigue that Lindbergh must have battled to stay alive.

The effects of sleep loss are well documented. A predictable irritability develops into a mental depression. Chronic sleeplessness will bring on hallucinations similar to LSD trips.

Elijah was a victim of sleep deprivation. He had overexerted himself by *running* nearly 120 *miles* from Carmel to Beersheba and then an extra day's worth into the Sinai desert! A great man of faith was reduced to despair—not from battle with the 450 prophets of Baal but from a simple skirmish with fatigue.

Never settle critical issues when tired. Get a good night's sleep and approach the issues with a fresh perspective.

Lord, help us learn from great Elijah's mistake.

And He is before all things, and in Him all things consist.
—COL. 1:17

When I was in high school, the only truly interesting topics to guys were girls, cars, and sports. Anything else was either boring or required for graduation.

But I had a good physics teacher. Mr. Wagner was tough, but he knew his stuff and taught in a way that made physics class interesting.

When we studied atomic structure, I struggled with the nucleus. Mr. Wagner said it was protons and neutrons packed together so tightly that splitting it was one form of atomic explosion. He said neutrons have no electrical charge and protons have a positive charge. I already knew that like charges repel and unlike charges attract, so theoretically the nucleus should fly apart, not stick together.

The textbook answer to this back then was that no one fully understood why the nucleus stuck together as it did.

I now believe that the true explanation for the nature of the nucleus is found in today's verse. Jesus Christ holds all things together.

Can you or I really hold our lives together without God's help?

> *Tribulation produces perseverance; and*
> *perseverance, character; and character, hope.*
> —ROM. 5:3–4

A close friend and I were recently commenting on what seemed to be a lack of character of many families in our area. We were particularly struck by the apparent influence that affluence seemed to have on many of the young people. We both commented how many individuals lose their identity in their pursuit of material attachments.

In thinking about this in light of today's Bible text, I am struck by how easy it is to take the above verses out of context. Many of our families are indeed suffering and persevering, but this doesn't seem to lead to hope and certainly not to character development. In order for me to have hope, I must have faith in Christ. If I believe in any way that my own efforts will eventually bring me hope I miss the mark every time.

Once again I must learn that in order to recover from my addiction to work and material security, I need relationships with God and my family and friends.

Lord, break my attachments to earthly security and increase my faith in you alone.

For to will is present with me, but how to perform what is good I do not find.   —ROM. 7:18

We do not usually recognize there is a problem until our lives become unmanageable. For the workaholic to feel life is unmanageable is to feel that the worst of sins has been committed. Yet the out-of-control workaholic will try to solve the problem by working harder. Such was the case with Carol. She was trying to have a meaningful career, keep a spotless home, and be the perfect spouse and mother. She began to lose control of all areas so she took what she thought to be the easiest course—she slept less and worked harder. Carol attempted to do it all and only had a disgruntled family and a case of depression to show for it.

Paul recognized that there was an element of his personality that became more unmanageable the more he tried to manage it. The result for him was greater discouragement and defeat. When Paul ceased fighting to gain control of his life and depended on God to carry him through, he was able to relax and regain management. It is good to know that as we accept our inability to manage, we become content.

Lord, help us to see beyond ourselves and trust you to deliver us.

> *And he will turn*
> *The hearts of the fathers to the children,*
> *And the hearts of the children to their fathers.*
> —MAL. 4:6

The idea of the importance of endings permeates our society. We talk about "the bottom line," "it's not over till it's over," and "when push comes to shove."

Spiritually, so much emphasis is placed on the last earthly words of Jesus Christ that they are commonly referred to as "The Great Commission" (Matthew 28:18–20).

Today's verse is also an ending. It is found at the very end of the entire Old Testament. When God was ready to sign off from his first written broadcast about himself, he did it with an announcement, a commercial if you will, regarding fathers and children.

If endings are so significant, and if God is making an awesome statement about the relationship between the hearts of fathers and children, then I have two questions for you and for myself.

Life is getting later. Do you know where your heart is? Do you know where the hearts of your children are?

In the fear of the LORD there is strong confidence,
And His children will have a place of refuge.
—PROV. 14:26

As you continue to work on your recovery you may notice the degree of distance that exists between you and your children. The older the child, the more difficult it will be for each of you to develop a sense of trust in each other.

I was reminded of how trust in our children develops in a recent conversation with a friend about our adolescent children. My friend told me that his daughter had recently asked permission to do something. He and his wife approved the plans because they knew they could trust their daughter's judgment. My wife and I had had the same experiences with our own sons. As we discussed this matter further with our friends we wondered why so many people struggle with trusting their children.

The difference, we decided, was that we spent so much time with our children that we knew how they thought and how they made decisions. Because of this we had faith in their abilities.

_____

Where are you unable to trust your children? Talk with them about this and pray for God's help in building trust.

> *"But take heed to yourselves, lest your hearts be
> weighed down with carousing, drunkenness, and
> cares of this life, and that Day come on you
> unexpectedly."*
> —LUKE 21:34

How do you develop an ulcer? Follow the advice of
Dr. William T. Gibb in the *Medical Annals of the District
of Columbia* (1970, pp. 96–97). He satirically suggests:

- Forget about everything but your job. It comes
  first and your family understands why you have
  no time for them.

- Work at the office weekends and holidays.

- Never turn down a request that might even
  remotely further your career. Accept all invita-
  tions to meetings, dinners, and work assignments.

- Don't waste time with recreation.

- Don't delegate responsibility. You can do it best.
  Carry the whole load.

- Never mind the doctors; you're as strong as an
  ox. Those height/weight charts do not apply to
  you.

The key ingredients for an ulcer are stress and care-
lessness. We are warned not to be overtaken by the
cares of this life so that we lose understanding.

Lord, help us to maintain this temple of yours.

Children's children are the crown of old men,
And the glory of children is their father.
—PROV. 17:6

They were both awesome, this father and son. But they were the epitome of the "good news/bad news" syndrome. From his boyhood this dad was marked for greatness. As a youth he was a champion of champions.

The son would have made any man proud to be his dad. Early on he showed compassion and concern, even if he was somewhat impulsive and strong-willed. Later in his life he showed his cunning by engineering a hostile takeover of all that his dad had built.

And what had dad been doing all his son's life? Nothing short of making his mark on history. He was gifted in administration, personal relationships, and communication. He had fought and won so many battles in his field that folk songs were written about him. And he gave his children every advantage that he had not had in his youth.

If you want to read about it, check out 2 Samuel 13—18. This father was King David; the son was Absalom, who stole his father's kingdom.

Perhaps David was so busy killing enemy giants that he failed to see the enemy he raised in his own household. Are you killing the right giants?

> *"I will be his Father, and he shall be My son; and I will not take My mercy away from him, as I took it from him who was before you."*
> —1 CHRON. 17:13

Did you know your dad? This was a question recently posed to me by a close friend who like myself had grown up in the fifties at what many consider the peak of the "American Dream." Although we both loved our dads we were struck by the price they had to pay to give us the benefits they didn't have growing up in the Depression.

Though we appreciated their hard work, what we wanted more was to get to know them. Now in hindsight we see that what we craved was relationship.

As we look to the future we grieve again, for now a similar process is developing in families where both father and mother spend large hunks of time at work to provide for material needs. The casualties of personhood and relationship could be even higher in the next generation if we don't face our addictions to work and other things.

———————

Ask yourself how well you knew your parents as people and how well your family knows you. Seek opportunities to share about yourself and to listen to others doing the same.

He said, "This is the rest with which
You may cause the weary to rest,"
And, "This is the refreshing";
Yet they would not hear.

—ISA. 28:12

A danger for recovering workaholics is the tendency to purposely take the hard road in life. They feel something noble by not taking the easy way through a task. Rod, a pastor, was such a person. He overextended himself by doing what he thought needed to be done—his way, of course. This included preparing sermons, managing money, typing the bulletin, and the list goes on and on. As he said, "If I don't do it, it will not get done." The truth was that the task had to be done *his way*, and he was the only one who could do it to his satisfaction.

Pastors are not the only ones who fall into the trap of guilt and martyrdom. Mothers are famous for it also. By taking on the burden of all responsibilities two tragedies unfold. One, the burden bearer burns out. Second, she fosters irresponsibility and selfishness in her children, thus stunting their growth. God never intended for us to carry the world on our shoulders.

Learn to rest in your weariness, and if there is an easier way to do the job, take it.

God specializes in grace, not guilt!

He restores my soul.
—PS. 23:3a

My dad is an architect/contractor. He designs and builds everything from million-dollar homes to small renovations. He has earned a reputation for quality work.

I grew up working for him in the construction industry. I learned a great deal from my dad, and he had strong opinions about remodeling. He preferred to build from scratch.

"The thing about remodeling," he would say, "is that before you can build you have to tear down."

Restoration can be tough.

We remodeled part of our home recently. Two rooms were changed into one. Walls had to be demolished. It was dusty and dirty, and we had to live in it. It took longer than we had expected. Not everything worked out exactly right. Restoration can be tough.

The verse from Psalm 23 makes an interesting assumption: we are each in need of restoration. Something new needs to be built into our lives, and the first step is that something old needs to be torn down.

Have you stopped to discern what part of your life God wants to remodel? Restoration can be tough.

"Therefore understand that the Lord your God is not giving you this good land to possess because of your righteousness, for you are a stiff-necked people."

—DEUT. 9:6

While playing with one of my boys I strained my neck and shoulder, which resulted in a stiff neck for several days.

The slightest movement to the left or right resulted in excruciating pain. Performing the simplest tasks became a chore. I had lost my flexibility and needed to turn my whole upper torso to look in another direction. If the phone rang and I forgot I was quickly reminded of my stiff-necked status. It was like having a heavy wooden yoke around my neck.

My kids told me I looked funny. No matter how much you try to disguise a stiff neck everyone knows.

Work addicts are stiff-necked in a sense. We suffer from the misconception that hard work will eventually solve all our problems. We have a difficult time responding to other needs in our lives because it is painful to look in that direction.

In spite of our nature, however, God still desires for us to recover from our injury and see as he sees.

Take some time today to look in other directions in spite of the pain.

> *But godliness with contentment is great gain.*
> —1 TIM. 6:6

I remember as a child I would read the label of the Carnation milk cans. They carried the motto "from contented cows." Now I understand the point that the milk company was trying to make—that good things come from being content.

Do you know the state of contentment? Very few people do. Too many of us spend our lives preparing for the bad times, unable to enjoy the good times. One of the great challenges we therapists have is helping anxious people to live in the here and now.

To be content means to rest in the circumstances as they are now, both good and bad. "Easy for you to say," you might say. It is not. People aren't born with a "content personality." Contentment is *learned*. Learning comes only through repetition, experience, and practice. It requires the patience not to run ahead of our abilities and the self-discipline not to compare ourselves to others.

Think about some of the positive elements of your life. Has God ever failed you?

Lord, thank you for the contentment that comes with godliness.

When I kept silent, my bones grew old
Through my groaning all the day long.
—PS. 32:3

We have all seen it. At one time or another we've been to some high school ball game where the scoreboard had a light or two out. Technology has yet to attain perfection.

But our body is actually an incredibly accurate scoreboard. And mine kept score on me recently. I thought I had a cavity. Hot or cold liquids on one tooth caused intense pain. So off to my dentist I ran.

And—no cavity. No cavity? How could this be? The pain was real. The dentist described it as an inflamed root, the result of grinding my teeth. "Are you under any pressure?" he asked.

My first answer was no. Then I began to do some counting. In addition to my normal responsibilities of husband and father, I had added things like writing this devotional, taking a college correspondence course, and doing some major remodeling on our house. And my body was keeping score. My body had to dissipate the pressure because I was not.

Is your body trying to tell you something? Do you know how not to internalize stress, pressure, or anger?

> *"For the promise is to you and to your children,*
> *and . . . as many as the Lord our God will call."*
> —ACTS 2:39

I have to constantly struggle to keep a healthy balance between my career and my family. My children have helped me maintain discipline in this area. I remember one particular incident about five years ago when I was feeling kind of stagnant in my career and the lure of success was chewing me up. I began to wonder what would have happened if I had not responded to God's call and instead had finished my original career plans to be an electrical engineer. It sure looked more lucrative at that time.

I remembered a story one of my boys told me when someone challenged him about how "successful" his father was. To some this kind of challenge can be intimidating, but he told me he calmly said, "All I know is, he is successful as a dad." He'll never know what an affirmation that was to me and how much it helped me to let go of my obsession to succeed.

Father, thank you for those simple events in life that remind us of where our priorities are. Keep my career motives pure of any ambitions that are not a part of your will.

Then David danced before the LORD with all his might. . . . David said to Michal, "It was before the LORD, who chose me . . . . Therefore I will play music before the LORD."   —2 SAM. 6:14, 21

A ritual has developed in America that has become familiar to sports fans. It is the after-victory coverage of the champions' locker room. To regard the hollering, champagne shooting, and chest pounding as irresponsible behavior is to miss the point. These athletes are experiencing the culmination of their extensive training and effort. They were under constant stress and now are letting off steam. If they didn't do it they would crack.

King David celebrated before the Lord who made him king, but he was criticized by his wife for behavior unbecoming a king. How about you?

We need to have purposeful celebrations as part of our life. In many ways we have lost the art of celebrating. We neglect the symbolism of the holidays; we trample over tradition and protocol.

Do you work too much? Are you so tired on festive occasions that you sit around listless? Are you accused of being boring? When was the last time you acted like a kid?

————————

Lord, help us to remember that you have created the good times to offset the bad times, and teach us to enjoy them!

> *You shall not hate your fellow-countryman in your heart; you may surely reprove your neighbor and shall not incur sin because of him.*
> —LEV. 19:17, NAS

Cathy knew how to keep her anger inside. And as expected the results were devastating. She struggled with authority figures, lost control of her weight, and had very few truly close friends.

Cathy was a suppressor. She could not allow her anger to see the light of day. Hurts and disappointments of long ago were still vivid in her mind's eye and those pictures would not go away.

How does a suppressor get angry? Cathy first had to recognize what her anger looked like and sounded like. Through years of practice she had learned to avoid that valid emotion.

Second, she had to learn that anger is neither good nor bad. It is what we *do* with our anger that is either right or wrong. Many messages from our culture and church tell us that anger is wrong. So Cathy had to give herself permission to be angry.

Recognizing anger and giving herself permission to be angry were only the beginning for Cathy. Have you done those two steps?

"Speak to the rock before their eyes, and it will yield its water. . . ." Then Moses lifted his hand and struck the rock twice with his rod; and water came out abundantly.
—NUM. 20:8, 11

Only two ways to do things existed: Cindy's way and the wrong way. Her husband was fed up. After five years of marriage he was ready to leave.

Cindy was an expresser. When it came to anger she had no hesitation about telling someone her own opinion. But to her it was not mere opinion, it was fact. She was like a volcano: others were frequently scalded with her burning lava, yet she suffered none of the ill effects of internalizing strong emotion.

Anger expressed incorrectly costs the expresser. Because Moses disobeyed and struck the rock out of his anger instead of speaking to it as commanded, he was disqualified from entering the promised land. Because Cindy was so intent on expressing her emotions she was on the verge of losing her mate.

The first step for Cindy was to recognize that a *carte blanche* expression of anger is not a better alternative than internalizing anger. She is beginning to examine her emotions before allowing them to erupt.

Where are you? Do you erupt all over those close to you?

February 1 – QUALITY AND QUANTITY TIME

> "LORD, make me to know my end,
> And what is the measure of my days,
> That I may know how frail I am."
> —PS. 39:4

Time is the one true commodity of family life which we all must struggle with in our recovery. My wife and I recently spent some valuable time with some friends who recently made a decision to leave the urban rat race, change careers, and move out of state.

One of the most striking lessons the father of this family has learned is the importance of quantity and quality time. Until he had new work he was looking forward to spending time with his children. It didn't take long, however, for him to become bored. His problem, he said, had to do with the misconception that all of his time with the children had to be productive quality time. When his children had other interests that did not include him he was confused at first. His puzzlement was lifted several months later, however, when the family was sitting around having an intimate chat at the end of the year. He realized that this quality time would not have taken place previously if it hadn't been for the long hours of quantity time spent with his children.

As work addicts used to being productive we need to realize that quality time occurs only after long hours of quantity companionship.

Let him kiss me with the kisses of his mouth—
For your love is better than wine.

—SONG 1:2

Dave works all the time!" Rhonda lamented. Dave was working two jobs and was the all-too-familiar absent father and husband. Rhonda was not finished with her story, however; with difficulty she moved directly to the point. "We had sex only twice last year, none this year. It has literally caused physical problems for me." She went on to explain in detail her disorder called pelvic congestion syndrome. It is the weakening of the ligaments around the cervix that is caused by a lack of sexual release.

Rhonda's problem is unusual. Dave's is not. The interesting thing is that Dave is not impotent. The real reasons for his sexual problem have not been uncovered at this point. He is certainly using work as the anesthetic to kill the pain and avoid facing the root causes.

When we consider what God has said about sexual intimacy between husbands and wives we realize that sex is not only appropriate, it is necessary for intimacy. Celebrate the God-given gift of your sexuality. He even says it is better than wine—and work, too!

Lord, help us not to call unclean what you have deemed clean.

> *And may the Lord make you increase and abound*
> *in love to one another and to all, just as we do*
> *to you.* —1 THESS. 3:12

One of the struggles of recovery when we give up our addiction to work is the void left in our identity. This is particularly true when we become aware of our need for relationship.

Charles had this kind of experience. He was hurt and angry that his family didn't want to spend time with him when he made an extra effort to leave the office on time. What he didn't realize at first was that his family was taking a wait-and-see attitude. They too were angry and hurt for the many years of not having their own needs met by him.

Charles eventually realized that he expected his family to meet his needs, to be emotionally open, and to be physically close. He eventually learned he was responsible for meeting his needs and could present them to others with no strings attached. He then discovered his family was more receptive and cooperative.

Father, please help me to understand the intensity of my need for others. Help me to relate without transferring my work addiction to an addiction to people.

But He gives more grace. Therefore He says:

> *"God resists the proud,*
> *But gives grace to the humble."*
> —JAMES 4:6

The Japanese auto industry introduced a new marketing concept to the United States and, unfortunately, the American auto makers have followed suit. It is called the preferred equipment package. The manufacturer sells various options as a package. If you want cruise control you may have to buy power seats and doors with it. Your power of choice is taken away. You must take it or leave it.

Workaholism dictates to us in a similar fashion. If we desire to overcome financial insecurity through overwork, we must take with it a package that may include illness, family problems, and disillusionment.

On the other hand, Scripture provides its own "preferred equipment package," the concept of *grace*. Grace is defined as *God giving me that which I do not deserve.* As we commit ourselves to him, he provides us with acceptance, forgiveness, purpose, security, joy, and fulfillment. He heals the emotional pain that is the cause of our workaholism. Grace is a preferred option we all can use!

Grace: God's riches at Christ's expense.

> *"He who formerly persecuted us now preaches the
> faith which he once tried to destroy."*
> —GAL. 1:23

James was prone to extremes. He had been raised in a
conservative atmosphere and had bought into those
principles and values. A man of considerable ability, he
had rightly earned high security clearance in our nation's military. He had married "correctly" a fine and
attractive woman.

But she was not the only good-looking woman in the
world, nor was she the only woman who looked more
than once at James. The problem was that James
looked back at some of those other women. And soon
he went from faithful husband to married man with a
mistress.

James's progress back to health was also "all or
nothing." There were weeks when his performance
was stellar, followed immediately by days when he totally blew it. His goal was simply to control his behavior, but he could not consistently do that. His hormones
eventually won over his self-control.

---

*The first step of recovery for James was to see that his behavior was a
result of extremes in his thinking and in his beliefs. How about you?
What are the extremes in your behavior and in your thoughts?*

*The weapons of our warfare are . . . casting down
arguments and every high thing that exalts itself
against the knowledge of God, bringing every
thought into captivity to the obedience of Christ.*
—2 COR. 10:4–5

In the "all-or-nothing" mode that was characteristic of
his life, James assumed both the problem and the solution lay in control of his actions. If he completely controlled his behavior, all was well. If he controlled
himself only partially, that was not enough and so why
try at all?

Initially he struggled with the difference between
having a thought and what that thought could do when
left unattended. Gradually he began to see that he
needed to govern his thoughts. Once he began to do
so, his actions began to become more manageable.

The Bible refers to this process as "bringing every
thought into captivity to the obedience of Christ." It is
not enough just to observe our thought processes. We
must confront our thoughts and challenge their validity by how they measure up to the standard of Jesus
Christ.

*What is your track record here? Just because you feel or think some-
thing, does that make it true?*

> *The righteous man walks in his integrity;*
> *His children are blessed after him.*
> —PROV. 20:7

Several years ago I made a conscious effort to spend more time with our sons. Most of this time was spent on some athletic pursuit, and our conversations were fairly superficial.

Recently my wife and I noticed that at the end of the day our sons, now both adolescents, will sit at the foot of our bed and share stories with us. Occasionally they will ask personal questions or present dilemmas they must make decisions about. Both of us feel this is occurring due to the amount of time I set aside for them over the past year.

It doesn't seem like that long ago that we were sitting at the foot of their beds reading or telling them bedtime stories to help them relax and fall asleep. We both feel privileged to have them do the same for us now.

It can be helpful to share thoughts and activities with each other at the end of the day as it unwinds you and helps you rest well. Ask God to help you learn to enjoy these times of light conversation.

*And when the donkey saw the Angel of the LORD,
she lay down under Balaam; so Balaam's anger
was aroused, and he struck the donkey with his
staff. Then the LORD opened the mouth of the
donkey, and she said to Balaam, "What have I done
to you, that you have struck me these three times?"*
—NUM. 22:27–28

My house is pretty smart for an inanimate object. I turned the toaster on while the coffee pot, microwave, stove, and lights were all on. As you anticipated, the circuit breaker threw. As a result I had to turn something off if I wanted toast. The breaker would not allow me to ignore it regardless of how many times I reset it. That simple yet sophisticated device sensed the overload of electrical current.

Our bodies are equipped with a system similar to the old-fashioned fuse system which could be overridden. We, too, can override our bodies' warning. We may feel the effects of stress through the loss of health and unless we compensate with rest we will fry our circuits. Learn a lesson from Balaam and his donkey today. Our bodies ask the same question: "What have I done to you, that you have struck me?" His donkey had enough common sense to stop when it sensed danger. Do you?

Dear Lord, slow me down.

Train up a child in the way he should go,
And when he is old he will not depart from it.
—PROV. 22:6

The dictionary defines common sense as "sound practical judgment that is independent of specialized knowledge, training, or the like." The more our society functions in codependent styles (which includes workaholism) the less of this we seem to have.

I have noticed a pattern whereby parents will often call for therapy for their two-year-old children who are misbehaving. Usually this is an indication that the parent is the one who is out of control.

A parent will often use the expression "the kids are driving me crazy" as a means of describing how he feels out of balance. Actually, as a work-addicted parent he has no reference point. Consequently, when his normal two-year-old child makes normal demands he doesn't know how to respond so he panics. He has a fear of failing as a parent, which can be a part of the same compulsive pattern.

If you are excessively anxious about the functioning of your child, you may be the one who is out of control.

Blessed is every one who fears the LORD,
Who walks in His ways.
When you eat the labor of your hands,
You shall be happy, and it shall be well with you.
—PS. 128:1

The man being interviewed by CNN was a CEO of a major conglomerate. He works endlessly and thrives on pressure. The interviewer asked, "What makes you run?" He said, "I grew up hearing from my father that I would never amount to anything. I've done this to prove the [blankety-blank] wrong." His anger propelled him to the top and kept him going.

In his book, *Healing Grace*, David Seamands said, "I have yet to counsel a performance-based and perfectionistic Christian who was not at heart an angry person." I agree. I have met many perfectionists who either do not recognize or admit to being angry. Somewhere in their experience they were taught that the expression of anger was wrong or dangerous. So they swallowed anger—and became performers to overcome it, hoping that they would finally gain the approval they desired so badly.

Lord, help us to remember that we are to walk in your ways and please you.

> *Brethren, I do not count myself to have apprehended; but one thing I do, forgetting those things which are behind and reaching forward to those things which are ahead.* —PHIL. 3:13

I don't smoke and never have, but many of my relatives did. Perhaps that is why I can remember so many old cigarette commercials. I wanted to see how they were tricked into burning up their money.

Do you remember the Pall Mall ad? As I recall it went something like this: "Over, under, around, and through, Pall Mall travels pleasure to you."

Over, under, around, and through. That actually has application to workaholics, who seemingly always have too many responsibilities. There is always another job to do, another call to make, or another job to redo better.

If anyone in Scripture looked like a workaholic it was the apostle Paul, the author of today's verse. Yet it was the apostle Paul who wrote, "One thing I do."

Today we say, "These twenty things I dabble in." Remember the phrase "Jack of all trades, master of none." I found that to be a misquote from a phrase of early American history: "Jack of all trades, master of *one.*"

Are you mastering or dabbling? Take time to check on it.

Only let your conduct be worthy of the gospel of Christ, so that whether I come and see you or am absent, I may hear of your affairs, that you stand fast in one spirit, with one mind striving together for the faith of the gospel.
                                        —PHIL. 1:27

My oldest son and his best friend spent an entire Sunday studying for a biology test. After hours of work they were frustrated and ready to throw in the towel.

Both my son and his friend are good students but are frustrated by the lack of free time they have for relaxation or fun. Suddenly it struck me that even our school system was pushing our children to succeed while missing the more meaningful aspects of life.

I joked with them that when I was in school they had the FHA (Future Homemakers of America), and the FFA (Future Farmers of America). I suggested that they start a new group called the FWA (Future Workaholics of America).

Seriously, however, I believe it is an important part of your recovery to be aware of the impact of political and educational decisions that contribute to fostering another generation of codependent individuals.

God, please help me see flaws in our political and educational structures that disable us and make us vulnerable to further addictions.

> *For I acknowledge my transgressions,*
> *And my sin is ever before me.*
> *Against You, You only, have I sinned,*
> *And done this evil in Your sight.*
> —PS. 51:3–4

It was a crime that contained all the elements of a trashy novel: murder, deceit, lust, betrayal, and adultery. An executive falls in love with an employee's wife while the employee is out in the field serving his boss. Unable to keep his eyes off the woman, the boss determines to have his way with her. He overpowers her, seduces her, and gets her pregnant. But her husband's commitment to her stands in the way. So the boss plans an "accident" and the employee is killed. The executive then comforts the widow in her grief and the rest is history.

Such scum is unworthy of redemption, yet he was redeemed. In fact, he is the author of today's verse. It was King David of Israel who was later labeled "a man after God's own heart." The key point to remember today is that David did not allow his guilt to keep him from coming back to God. He faced what he had done and went to the only person who could help him now, remarkably the one he had ultimately betrayed: his God.

_____

Lord, help us to run to you at the time we feel most like running from you.

Better is a little with the fear of the LORD,
Than great treasure with trouble.

—PROV. 15:16

Perry had attended West Point and excelled in virtually everything. When he graduated the Army offered him his pick of top-rate opportunities. His tour of duty was filled with awards and he enjoyed it. Since he required only three or four hours of sleep a night, he added a few projects to his life.

He got an MBA, having made straight A's. When he left the Army, he found so many job openings that he had to prioritize the interviews.

He soon married and had two children. Still he stayed busy. Perry and his wife often went to bed together and then when she was asleep he would go to his desk to work. Work days were long, but he still tried to spend a little time with the family.

They came for counseling because his wife had an affair. He had been absolutely faithful, but life had become unbearable for her. He was a master at prioritizing projects but neglected to prioritize the relationships in his life. Perry had indeed accomplished much, but in many ways he had done nothing.

―――――――――

How balanced are your priorities?

> *But when He saw the multitudes, He was moved*
> *with compassion for them, because they were*
> *weary and scattered, like sheep having no*
> *shepherd.*
> —MATT. 9:36

The first step in recovery for Perry was to face the runaway lifestyle his need to excel demanded. There were tough questions that only he could answer. Why did he need to stay so active? What did he get from what he did? Why did he give more attention to his activities than to his closest relationships?

The realization for him was that in spite of all his outstanding accomplishments, achievements, and abilities, he was basically insecure. But he endeavored to prove his security and establish his worth through achievement in the outside world. His incredible ability actually worked against him. His gifts were a facade that seemingly covered the fact that he was a needy person.

Because we are a part of "the multitudes," we are needy, regardless of our abilities. Yet God views our distress with great compassion.

I would have lost heart, unless I had believed
That I would see the goodness of the LORD
In the land of the living.
Wait on the LORD*;*
Be of good courage,
And He shall strengthen your heart.
                              —PS. 27:13–14

In trying to teach my sixteen-year-old son to drive I have been reminded of one of the difficulties of recovery—learning new skills.

He stalled the car over and over as he tried to learn to coordinate the clutch and gas pedals. As he mastered this we would add new skills. When these new skills were added he discovered he could not concentrate on the old skill and we would have to start over.

In recovery we often expect to make continual progress. We forget that most new learning takes place with many trials and errors. How many times did we fall when we learned to walk or ride a bike?

Remember how you learned to ride a bike, swim, skate, or drive a car. Think about each step you took to learn, including those frustrating times when you didn't progress.

> *For you did not receive the spirit of bondage again*
> *to fear, but you received the Spirit of adoption by*
> *whom we cry out, "Abba, Father."*
>
> —ROM. 8:15

Imagine what it must have been like to grow up with a father who beat you to the point that you required hospitalization. Add to that the psychological pain of being infertile due to a birth defect, a point emphasized by your father who is resentful because he won't have grandchildren. Such is the story of Donnie, who had come for counseling because his wife had left him. She loved him deeply but could not live with his uncontrolled spending and lying to cover it up. Donnie also works incessantly but his spending seems to outdistance his income.

Donnie recognizes that the reason for overworking is to hear his father praise him. The reason for his overspending is to appear successful to Dad. Donnie has finally realized that he will never have his dad's approval. Donnie must replace his need for his father's approval with the understanding that he is already approved by God, his heavenly Father. This feeling can come only as he experiences acceptance from the people who love him now and through visitation with God.

———————

Lord, thank you for your acceptance; help us to see you as "Dad."

*For the Spirit searches all things, yes, the deep
things of God.* —1 COR. 2:10

Rich was reluctant about seeing me for therapy but did so at his wife's suggestion. She had separated from him about four months earlier and he was frustrated that she hadn't returned home. He admitted he needed some help to understand why she left so that he could get her back.

As Rich and I met weekly it became obvious his wife had told him many times why she had left. He showed me letters she had written where she described being second fiddle to his private company and hating his abuse of her and their children.

When I tried to discuss her unhappiness with Rich he justified his actions. He said it was hard to keep the business going that he inherited from his father. He said his wife had always been financially secure, had a very nice home, and had plenty of clothes to wear.

Rich was still in denial. As we explored his background in more detail I learned he worked as much as sixty to seventy hours per week in his company. But Rich couldn't see how his work addiction was a problem.

Lord, give me eyes to see and ears to hear the ignorance of my actions.

> *I cry out to the LORD with my voice;*
> *With my voice to the LORD I make my supplication.*
> *I pour out my complaint before Him;*
> *I declare before Him my trouble.* —PS. 142:1–2

Rich had now been in therapy three months. He was beginning to come out of his denial, and he was angry at me because I wasn't telling him how to get his wife back. To compound his situation he had developed cancer, which increased his expectations that his wife would come home. When he was in denial he lived with the hope that his wife would return home when the money ran out. In fact, she had secured a very good job and was living comfortably.

Now out of denial, Rich lost control. He now blamed me for not having answers. We spent the next several months addressing his anger and his need to be in control. Rich had to overcome anger because all his hard hours of work had actually resulted in his losing instead of keeping the one he loved. The harder he worked to get her back the less progress he made. Rich was slowly learning to let go.

Workaholics often believe that hard work is the only way they can have love. Take inventory of current and past relationships to determine where you have been loved with no strings attached.

Those who sow in tears
Shall reap in joy.
He who continually goes forth weeping,
Bearing seed for sowing,
Shall doubtless come again with rejoicing.
—PS. 126:5–6

Rich's cancer was getting progressively worse. However, he had progressed well in his emotional recovery. He had traced the roots of his anger to his family of origin for the unrealistic expectations they placed on him as a child. He also realized he never really wanted to take over his father's business.

As he continued to let go he was overcome with grief. First, for the ideal parents he would never have and now for the guilt over the pain inflicted on his wife and children.

Rich's wife had been living out of state. He had made several visits to see her, but not once did she come and see him, even during a brief hospital stay.

Rich was learning to love her unconditionally. That included the toughest love of all—loving her enough not to expect her to return home. This was the most difficult part of a successful recovery. He had to let go completely and trust God for the future.

God, comfort me in these times of deep sorrow and help me trust you to be my hope.

> *There is therefore now no condemnation to those*
> *who are in Christ Jesus.*
> —ROM. 8:1

Behind every successful man stands a mother-in-law who is saying he will never amount to anything." As in most tongue-in-cheek quips there is a kernel of truth beneath the humor. There seems to be a negative motivator behind many ambitious people, particularly perfectionists/workaholics. The negative motivator may be a critical parent, teacher, or sibling. The most popular image is of God himself, who is represented as the celestial policeman standing aloof with arms folded. This image is always present in our minds, reminding us that we must never fail or we will be met with disapproval.

How different a picture of God is formed when you consider this verse as the starting point! Nowhere is it written that we must perform to earn his approval. If you know him personally he pronounces that there is no condemnation on you. He knew you would have a difficult enough time trying to work through all the requirements that you placed on yourself. To know that you can never fall out of his love frees you to perform without the risk of rejection if you fail.

Lord, thank you for this wonderful verse. Help us to remember it when we feel condemned.

Husbands, love your wives and do not be bitter toward them.
—COL. 3:19

Jason and Candy were a striking couple. Both were well educated and accomplished in their chosen careers. Each had established a personal relationship with Jesus Christ at an early age and both had continued to nurture that relationship. They had been married for four years, but they had separated after only three months.

It was the first marriage for both. Neither had had affairs and neither had even dated during their separation. Divorce was not an option to them at first, though they were considering it now. Each blamed the other for the continued separation.

Jason had a picture of what his marriage would look like, what God would do in his marriage, and how his wife would respond to him. It was not a bad picture, it was just not realistic. When he saw that he could not make reality look like his image, he bolted.

How different does your marriage appear from what you had anticipated? How has that changed your view of your mate and your marriage?

> *For the flesh lusts against the Spirit, and the Spirit*
> *against the flesh . . . so that you do not do the*
> *things that you wish.*   —GAL. 5:17

Jason struggled for control of his life. It was not that he didn't want to control Candy, but he did want to control how his life and marriage looked.

Jason could not admit that there was a problem in his marriage; that would mean admitting that either he was a bad husband or that he had married the wrong woman. He was too insecure to admit he was a faulty husband. But if he had married the wrong woman then something was wrong with him for making such a lousy choice.

All roads led back to the same conclusion: something's wrong with Jason. But in reality, his dysfunction was that he thought he could control his life. He did not know there is strength in powerlessness. It took him six months to discover that it is from weakness that he could actually derive strength. Only when he admitted weakness did everything *not* depend on him or his mate.

Jason had to find out the hard way that he was not God and was not supposed to control everything.

———————

Lord, give me the wisdom to see that you are God and I am not.

Have mercy on me, O LORD, for I am in trouble;
My eye wastes away with grief,
Yes, my soul and my body!   —PS. 31:9

Part of Candy's problem in this marriage was not so different from Jason's. The primary difference was that she was the "hurtee" and not the "hurter." She was grieving, even as the verse today describes. She had been rejected by the person to whom she had made herself most vulnerable. The reasons were not even clear and the accusations were shaky, to say the least.

Her primary difficulty lay in an inability to step away and let something that hurt tremendously belong to someone else. She took Jason's "flaw" personally because it was directed at her. She tried to control his treatment of her, which only kept him at arm's length.

It is difficult to let go of control when we are in pain; our instinct for self-preservation makes us want to *do* something. But again, only when we acknowledge our vulnerability and call out to God as David did will we truly experience comfort.

––––––––––––––

Lord God, thank you for being aware of my pain and looking upon it with compassion and grace.

*Therefore, if anyone is in Christ, he is a new
creation: old things have passed away; behold,
all things have become new.* —2 COR. 5:17

Is it possible to be a success in business and not be a
workaholic?" Dan asked. He had come for counseling
because his wife was ready to leave and his kids were
behavior problems. Dan had been oblivious to it all because he was seldom home.

In reference to his question I told Dan about another
Dan, whom we will refer to as Dan Two. Dan Two is
the president of a successful finance company. He has
an estate and drives a late model Mercedes. In the standards of the world, Dan Two is successful. What is
unique about Dan Two is that he is home every night
by six, is actively involved in his church, and values
the time spent with his family. It has not always been
this way, however; it took him three failed marriages
and a battle with alcohol to bring him to his senses.
Now, at fifty years old Dan Two has finally set the
proper boundaries and is a self-proclaimed recovering
workaholic.

The beauty of dedicating our lives to Christ is the
fact that we can see real change in what is a seemingly
hopeless situation.

Lord, thank you for making us new, day by day.

A soft answer turns away wrath,
But a harsh word stirs up anger.
—PROV. 15:1

Beth was fourteen. Her parents had brought her for counseling because of her "defiant" attitude. In private Beth told me she was angry at her father for his high expectations of her and the family. She was also angry at her mother because she expected her and her sister to comply with his expectations. She vividly remembered the day she decided she couldn't take it anymore.

She was at the mall with her parents and sister shopping for clothes. This was never a pleasant experience. If she expressed an interest in something outside the family's price range or spent too much time window shopping he would threaten not to buy her anything. When they stopped for lunch at the food court, her father wanted everyone to get the same thing to save time. It was a very busy day and when they went to look for a seat her father started to yell at her and her sister for not getting a table soon enough. When Beth saw some of her school friends nearby snickering she was so enraged she lost it. For the first time she started screaming right back.

Think about the expectations you have of others. Ask God to help you see where you are being unrealistic.

> *Behold, how good and how pleasant it is*
> *For brethren to dwell together in unity!*
> *It is like the precious oil upon the head.*
> —PS. 133:1–2

After the incident at the mall Beth decided she didn't care anymore. Although her parents were appalled to discover she had begun to see a nineteen-year-old high school senior, this young man treated her just the opposite of her father. He took her places and bought her nice gifts.

What scared her parents were the age difference and the young man's intentions. They legitimately feared their young daughter's vulnerability and were threatening to press charges if Beth continued to see him.

In family therapy Beth continued to challenge and defy any suggestion her father made about her judgment. I encouraged her to discuss her anger. Eventually, after several months of treatment, she was able to get through to her father. He cut back on his work and spent more time getting to know his daughter.

Beth's father, like many workaholics, was destroying family life by imposing unrealistic controls. In this case Beth transferred her needs for an ideal father to another because she felt betrayed and abandoned by her real father.

_____

If you have memories like the above, ask God to help you back off from the control and ask for forgiveness.

*For I say, through the grace given to me, to
everyone who is among you, not to think of himself
more highly than he ought to think, but to think
soberly, as God has dealt to each one a measure
of faith.*
—ROM. 12:3

One of the most painful experiences we can face is to
have our inadequacies exposed for all to see. A famous
baseball player was recently released from jail. He
served a five-month sentence for income tax evasion.
On top of that he was banned from baseball for life for
gambling on the game he loved so much. He had in
essence owned the city in which he played ball, but
now he was subjected to the anger of the people he had
let down.

It's easy to understand how a person who is given
extraordinary privileges throughout the course of his
life soon begins to feel entitled to them. It is said of Pete
Rose that upon his conviction he was the most surprised, for he had never before had to suffer the consequences of his actions. Let us not be pompous, because
we are no different. We can take advantage of the
grace of God and act entitled, because we do indeed
have a special place with him. The key is that he loves
us too much to let us get away with it.

Lord, help us not to think of ourselves too highly.

> *Be still, and know that I am God;*
> *I will be exalted among the nations,*
> *I will be exalted in the earth!*
> —PS. 46:10

Recently someone described an exceptional football player: "He always has his motor running at full speed." That is an accurate description of Kay. The idea that she should "be still and know," as the psalm said, was as foreign to her as it would have been to a two-year-old child.

She always had something else that needed to be done. If she could have figured out some way to shift into fast forward she would have.

Perfectionists need to accomplish a lot. The confounding part of it is that for every one accomplishment, at least two more projects appear in its place. Kay worked hard and efficiently, much more so than those around her. It was not so much that she got behind, as that she never got ahead. There was always someone who demanded her attention.

The harder she ran, the harder she needed to run. It took her several months to conclude that *since* there would always be more to do, she needed to revitalize herself by being still and knowing that God was God and she was "just" Kay.

Have you discovered your need to be still and let God be God?

When pride comes, then comes shame;
But with the humble is wisdom.
—PROV. 11:2

I like to play a game with my students that goes like this: "What is the first thing that you think of when you think of Samson?" "Delilah" would be the most likely response. The object of the game is to show that we often neglect the most important elements of the story.

Let's try it: What is the first thing that comes to mind when you think of pride? Arrogance? Haughtiness? Destruction? Boasting? Conceit? Now, these would all be good answers because Scripture abounds with verses supporting them. However, there is one type of pride that is seldom identified, and it is often more destructive, yet more subtle, than the other types. It is the pride of perfectionism. Perfectionism is often seen as a noble gesture—you want to do your best. There is nothing wrong with that. But when *wanting* to be perfect is replaced with a *demand* to be perfect, it indicates an intolerance and denial of your own frailties and weaknesses. It is an unwillingness to accept in yourself what God has long recognized and accepted—your sinfulness. Now that's pride!

_____

Lord, give us the courage to see ourselves as you see us.

> *And I testify again to every man . . . that he is a*
> *debtor to keep the whole law.* —GAL. 5:3

Having a workaholic perspective on life creates traps that appear to be solutions instead of problems. The most common of these traps is the "List System."

At one time or another, each of us has made a list in an effort to be more efficient. Very likely, many of us do so on a regular basis. We have our "paper brains"— our appointment book, planning calendar, and so on. Quite frankly, businesses and homes would be in far worse condition without the use of tools like this.

But there are different ways to use the same tool. I can take a hammer and build a table. Or I can take the same hammer and break someone's window. The same is true of our use of lists. It is the *system* aspect of lists that can blindside us.

Try this exercise. On a sheet of paper write down the various "hats" that you typically wear—father or mother, employee or employer, neighbor, son or daughter, and so on. Once you have those categories, ask yourself things, like, "What should a good father do?" How about a "good daughter"? Then ask yourself how you are doing at fulfilling these roles.

Do you have a list or is it a law?

For as many as are of the works of the law are
under the curse; for it is written, "Cursed is
everyone who does not continue in all things which
are written in the book of the law, to do them."
—GAL. 3:10

What did you notice from your own lists? Did any categories take precedence over the others? Was the source of your list intrinsic or extrinsic? Did the list come from what you chose to do or what someone else chose for you?

Some people look at their lists and responsibilities and say something like, "I've got to try hard. I've got to make sure to use my time and talents wisely."

It is from this chosen response pattern that we find our "producers," our entrepreneurs, our professional people, our clergy, and yes, our counselors and therapists. The *system* dictates that I must do these things well if I am to be of value. If I do not reach a high standard of performance then my contribution is not acceptable.

The pitfall is that according to the *system* aspect (and even endorsed by Scripture) if this is the way I am going to live, then I must perform flawlessly in every category.

How does your performance level measure? To yourself? To your mate? To your boss? How hard are you working?

Christ has redeemed us from the curse of the law,
having become a curse for us (for it is written,
"Cursed is everyone who hangs on a tree").
—GAL. 3:13

Suppose that on a woman's list is the notation that she should have a good figure. Following the system, she will exercise and diet in order to attain that goal. She can probably do quite well, for a while. Then someone whose body is better proportioned comes along and the standard changes. And the woman can no longer achieve her goal.

At this point a person will revert to the second way of responding to his list. Instead of "trying hard," now it becomes "I give up." Since she can no longer perform adequately, the only option left is to quit.

We can express that mentality, either passively or actively. The passive person looks at the list and says, "I cannot do this, and if I try everyone will know I'm a failure, so I just will not try anymore." The active responder looks at the list and says, "Whether or not I do what is there does not make me a valuable person, so I am going to intentionally reject the things on the list." Teenagers often react to their parents' lists for them like this.

———————

Where are you? Are you trying hard? Are you giving up, actively or passively?

He is a double-minded man, unstable in all
his ways.
                                    —JAMES 1:8

Just as it is impossible to stay indefinitely on the "try hard" side of the system, neither is it possible to remain on the "give up" side. Both sides get old. And the people who sell package vacations make their living on that fact.

The fact is, even if I am able to maintain the "try hard" side for a long period of time, it drives me toward burnout. Thus, I need to get away. Usually, we call this break from the system a vacation.

But the workaholic cannot stand much more than even one week of vacation. Too much nonproductive time drives the workaholic up a wall. So after choosing to be in the "give up" mode for a short period of time, he reverts back to the "try hard" mentality until he needs another break. And then the cycle starts all over again.

How did the hippies of the sixties and seventies respond to the "lists" of their parents' establishment? Did they not "give up"? But what do we call yesterday's hippies? Are they still driving old VW vans and living in communes? No. Yesterday's hippie is today's yuppie, driving a BMW, working for a Fortune 500 company, and "trying hard."

What goes around comes around. Locate yourself. Where are you? Could you use some stability you cannot find?

> *Be anxious for nothing, but in everything by prayer*
> *and supplication, with thanksgiving, let your*
> *requests be made known to God.* —PHIL. 4:6

Before drawing some solution-oriented conclusions about this List System, we should point out some telltale emotions.

In the "try hard" mode one particular emotion stands out: anxiety. When the workaholic or perfectionist is trying hard there is always the risk that he will not do something well enough, or thoroughly enough, or at the right time, or under budget, or any number of other concerns. Thus all the ingredients are in place for anxiety to grow and flourish.

On the other hand, the "give up" mode carries its own characteristic emotion: anger. The one who passively gives up is angry because of an artificial standard that implies false things about him. The one who actively gives up is angry because a standard of performance he does not want is being forced upon him.

Are you a member of AA—the Anger and Anxiety Club? Does either of these emotions describe the bulk of your emotional experience? If so, then the List System has you in its grasp.

Therefore we conclude that a man is justified by faith apart from the deeds of the law.
—ROM. 3:28

The List System rewards the doers, and it usually eats them up in the process.

Consider Tamara. She came to counseling to resolve a very painful past. But she was superb in her job. She did so well that the office manager designated her as the unit trainer, an important position.

Then she became ill. Her therapy was going extremely well, but this problem was medical. And no one knew about it. All that was evident was that she was slipping on the job. She who had once been the master trainer was now making elementary mistakes. Within two months her manager was considering letting her go. She was no longer an asset to the company. Her performance had slipped and she became expendable.

The principle works in both directions. Back when Tamara was excelling, the company actually bribed her to stay with them. We call such a bribe a raise. Such is the nature of the List System. Its rewards and punishments are based solely on performance.

To what extent do you operate in this system? Do you believe that God treats us according to this system?

> *But God demonstrates His own love toward us, in*
> *that while we were still sinners, Christ died for us.*
> —ROM. 5:8

With the List System, our performance alone determines our value. It shows up in businesses, marriages, churches, families, government, and virtually any place where there are interpersonal relationships.

This system is both the ladder the workaholic climbs to the top and the greased slide that takes him even more quickly to the very bottom.

But the Scriptures indicate that God operates on a very different system. In fact, his system is in diametrical opposition to the List System. In today's verse there is a portrait of our performance: "while we were sinners." According to God's standards, our performance stunk.

The verse also portrays his assessment of our value: "Christ died for us." In spite of our poor performance, God declares that we are of such incredible worth that he paid the highest price he possibly could, the life of his Son, to purchase us.

Dear God, help me to see my worth through your eyes. And help me see the worth and value of others in that same perspective. Help me to begin to grasp unconditional love and acceptance.

*For we are His workmanship, created in Christ
Jesus for good works, which God prepared
beforehand that we should walk in them.*
—EPH. 2:10

Darryl became sullen when he first grasped the implications of the List System. He was a high-ranking executive whose position demanded that he work hard, long, and effectively. His practice of determining worth and value on the basis of performance meant that he would have to start viewing work as a liability.

But the Scriptures again give the correct perspective on worth. *Workmanship* in today's verse literally means "masterpiece." Michelangelo's paintings in the Sistine chapel are not masterpieces because of what they do but because of what they are.

God did not plan for us to derive our basic significance from our work though he still wants us to work in significant ways. But we are already significant because of our relationship to him.

When Darryl realized that his worth, value, and significance were not dependent upon his performance at work, he was freed from the tremendous pressure to perform. As a result, his performance actually improved.

_____

How much of your value comes from what you do? How much comes from what you are?

> *Therefore, my beloved brethren, let every man be*
> *swift to hear, slow to speak, slow to wrath.*
> —JAMES 1:19

One of the most difficult skills to develop is the ability to listen. There are practical things you can do to develop this ability.

First, work on being attentive. I find it helpful to look directly at the other person. Tell the family member who is talking to you that you are trying to listen. Tell her to let you know if she thinks you're daydreaming.

Second, pay attention to tone of voice or facial expressions to give you clues about what they're feeling. When you pay attention to feelings it lets the other person know you care.

Third, try to monitor your own feelings so as not to have them unconsciously send another message to your speaker. If the feelings are too intense, confess them gently and ask for a "time-out" from listening until you can control them.

If you practice this regularly you will slowly get to know your family and develop deeper relationships.

God, I confess I am a poor listener. Give me ears to hear those in my family.

For you were once darkness, but now you are light in the Lord. Walk as children of light.

—EPH. 5:8

The marker board was filled with the list of duties Lynn had performed in her church before she suffered from major depression. Now at a healthy state of recovery, she was looking forward to reinvolvement in some kind of service. Her greatest fear was that she would again get overinvolved. Lynn had been the model woman—a faithful mother, wife, and church member. She felt the pressure to be perfect, and out of pride, she refused to admit that she was crumbling inside.

Lynn was now at the critical point of setting new boundaries. She had come through the crisis of admitting that she needed to set boundaries for herself, a thought that was new to her. Now was the time to experiment, to find out what her new limits would be. First, Lynn had to recognize the attitudes that caused the problem in the first place. Second, she had to identify her weak spots (for Lynn, it was the difficulty of saying no). Finally, she had to recognize her motives for overperforming.

Old boundaries are passing away; all boundaries are becoming new.

> *"For as the rain comes down, and the snow from*
>   *heaven,*
> *And do not return there,*
> *But water the earth,*
> *And make it bring forth and bud. . . ."*
> —ISA. 55:10

Tony was a very competent doctor, but he lived with the constant fear that he would lose all his patients and face financial ruin. Because of this he always over-booked his appointments, and he ignored advice from his partners and family to slow down. He got especially anxious during snow days.

What Tony hated most about snow days was that he couldn't control them. He felt obligated to make them up to his patients.

His children didn't help his disposition. They were excited that school had been canceled for the day and hoped that Dad would help them build a snowman. Secretly he envied those fathers who weren't prisoners of their jobs as he was. He often fantasized that things would be better if he had not gotten into this profession, but he knew some of his own peers seemed to have more flexibility in their lives.

When I become excessively anxious about things out of my control, I need to back off and reevaluate.

Then Nathan said to David, "You are the man! . . ."
David said to Nathan, "I have sinned against
the Lord."
                                             —2 SAM. 12:7, 13

Six words are seldom spoken, but when they are, magic can come. The words are, "You are right; I was wrong." Have you ever considered what it takes to say those words? Let me give you a clue from Step Ten of the Twelve Step program: "Continued to take personal inventory, and when we were wrong, promptly admitted it."

To take personal inventory, we must first be willing to admit our tendency to repress painful thoughts. Second, we must find the courage to face those painful experiences. Third, we must be willing to admit our part in the problem and the solution.

One of the leading motivators of workaholism is the avoidance and repression of pain and responsibility. The workaholic buries his pain in his work, hoping the distraction will make the pain go away.

The hard part of this step is the last: "when we were wrong, promptly admitted it." Pride and the pain of humiliation keep us from admitting wrong. As long as we are concerned about these two issues we will be held captive by them. David knew enough about himself and God to know that he would never find peace until he did the hardest thing—admit he was wrong and be reconciled.

_____

Say it three times: You were right; I was wrong.

> *Have mercy on me, O LORD, for I am weak;*
> *O LORD, heal me, for my bones are troubled.*
> —PS. 6:2

Most of us with work addictions have been conditioned to believe emotions are a sign of weakness so we deny our feelings. As the numbness of denial wears off we begin to feel a variety of emotions.

Emotions function like the control panel on your automobile. When a red light comes on you stop as soon as possible to see what the problem is. Not being in touch with your emotions would be like disconnecting the power to the control panel and running the risk of breakdown without warning.

This phase of recovery is traumatic because we begin to realize how out of control we have been. It is often paradoxical, because we must lose control to gain control again. Explore these feelings with a friend or counselor who acknowledges them and accepts you. Your emotions will seem less scary and will become your own radar for learning how to respond to life. Your hope and confidence will build as you realize you are free to share your feelings.

God, thank you for the gift of my emotions. Help me to be open to sharing them with you.

The LORD upholds all who fall,
And raises up all those who are bowed down.
—PS. 145:14

Often the thought of sharing feelings with our immediate family brings a sense of hopelessness. "They can't help." "They won't understand." "They will reject or ridicule me." These thoughts may have some truth to them but that is still no reason for not trying to share. Reconciliation can occur only in an atmosphere of openness and acceptance.

We must first identify our feelings in preparation for sharing. Think of the following feelings: sad, happy, angry, and scared. Ask yourself what things in your life trigger these feelings.

Next, when sharing always start your sentences with "I." This is to help keep that focus on you and minimize blame of others.

Sharing is most effective if the listener wants to listen and is attentive. Try to be sensitive to others if they don't care to listen right away, but don't deny your feelings to yourself. Make a point to talk about it later.

God, help me share my feelings with those I love, and help my family learn to accept me as you do.

> *Stand fast therefore in the liberty by which Christ*
> *has made us free, and do not be entangled again*
> *with a yoke of bondage.*   —GAL. 5:1

Is it not peculiar that the apostle Paul would have to admonish us to stand fast in our *liberty?* Would it not be something that we would naturally guard with our lives? It is difficult to imagine a nation willing to give up its freedom in order to escape the rigors of responsibility liberty requires, but it does happen.

A graphic example of this occurrence was Nazi Germany. Erich Fromm wrote a book on the Nazi phenomenon entitled *Escape from Freedom.* Why did the German people give up their liberty? They obviously did not intend to. The country was in a depression and they took the easiest approach—they believed the promises of a madman.

We can see the same dynamics taking place in our own lives. By nature we do not want to take the difficult trail; if there is an easier way we will take it. However, we pay a price in the loss of control, the loss of freedom. If we are overworked and overburdened by the problems of life, we may be too distracted to notice our control over the important matters slipping.

Vigilance is the eternal price of liberty.

He is despised and rejected by men,
A Man of sorrows and acquainted with grief.
And we hid, as it were, our faces from Him;
He was despised, and we did not esteem Him.
—ISA. 53:3

Dan was lost in the experience he had had as a twelve-year-old boy when he rode the bus to his new school. He still felt the torment of the kids who had chosen him as the object of their ridicule. They laughed at his size, they stole his hat, they made jokes about his mother.

But what hurt the most was the memory that he never fought back. It haunts him. He has determined never to be in that position again.

Now he overreacts at the slightest provocation, ready to fight for his dignity. He drives himself at work to prove to himself that he is just as good as his peers. He is trying to drive away that scared little boy who only needs a hug and encouragement. He has become the recipient of the shame the bullies carried about.

Dan needed to know also that he was in good company. The subject of today's verse is the Son of God. Jesus was despised and rejected by people who had only shame to share with him. He was able to respond with love and acceptance.

———————

Lord, thank you for loving us in spite of the pain we cause you.

> *So Pharaoh commanded all his people, saying,*
> *"Every son who is born you shall cast into the river,*
> *and every daughter you shall save alive."*
>
> —EX. 1:22

Today will begin a six-day study of how some of the events in the life of Moses led to workaholic tendencies.

In today's text we learn about some of the events early in Moses' life. The new pharaoh was threatened because the Israelite population was growing faster than his own and he feared losing control of his kingdom. In an effort to control this he placed the Israelites into slavery in hopes this would reduce their numbers. When this didn't work he issued an order to drown all male infants in the Nile. When Moses was born he was hidden for three months by his parents, but eventually he was placed in a basket and floated down the Nile.

As the story progresses Moses was rescued by the pharaoh's daughter and given back to his sister to nurse for her. After he was weaned, Moses was returned to the pharaoh's daughter and became her son.

Think about the impact on young Moses, to go from the loving and nurturing arms of his own family to the foster care of a family that was rife with control problems and fear.

*So she had compassion on him, and said, "This is
one of the Hebrews' children."*
—EX. 2:6

Moses was raised by the daughter of the ruler who
ordered his death. We are told she felt sorry for the
infant and decided to raise him on her own.

What was the pharaoh's daughter like? She had compassion, but what impact did her father's control and
tyranny have on her and the way she nurtured and
guided Moses? Who was his foster father and what
kind of a role model was he? How did his mother deal
with the issue of Moses' heritage?

We can only speculate at these and other questions
but by observing Moses' behavior in later life we can
deduce that the example of his foster family left Moses
feeling insecure about his identity and his destiny.

Work addicts, like other codependents, often come
from backgrounds where anger, control, and power
are frequently out of balance. The Scriptures indicate
that behavioral traits will be repeated from one generation to the next if they have gone unchecked.

*Pray to understand how your current functioning is to some degree a
product of your past.*

> *So he looked this way and that way, and when he*
> *saw no one, he killed the Egyptian and hid him in*
> *the sand.*
> —EX. 2:12

Moses saw some of his Israelite ancestors being beaten by an Egyptian slavemaster and became angry. After checking to see if anyone was watching he killed the Egyptian and buried him to hide any evidence. In this incident we see the turmoil that must have raged inside Moses as he was being raised in the family of the pharaoh. We also see the violent example set by his foster grandfather the pharaoh.

To make the tragedy worse the following day Moses witnessed two Israelites physically fighting and questioned them.

The two slaves confronted Moses, asking where he got the authority to ask them such a question. For the second time in his life he was rejected by his own blood and it stirred fear in him should the matter become known to his foster grandfather the pharaoh. Eventually the pharaoh did hear of the matter and wanted to kill Moses.

This drove Moses, fearing death, into the land of Midian.

Workaholics like Moses are driven by unseen emotions. What emotions lie buried within you?

But [Moses] said, "O my Lord, please send by the hand of whomever else You may send."

—EX. 4:13

If we look back earlier in the life of Moses we notice very early signs of a poor self-image. His response to God's command in Exodus 3:11 is "Who am I, that I should go to Pharaoh and bring the Israelites out of Egypt?"

This is no problem for God, who immediately reassures him that "I will be with you. . . ." But we see as the story continues that Moses in his doubt continues to question God's judgment, being concerned that the Israelites will not believe him. God in each case tells Moses how to respond. But Moses then resists the command further by debating his lack of eloquence as a speaker. God at this point must remind him of who made his mouth able to speak in the first place. Moses still resists and tells God, "O Lord, please send someone else to do it."

Because of these insecurities Moses was probably afraid of failure and believed he must always be in control. This may have been due to unresolved feelings from earlier in his life and his unresolved fear for how he had left Egypt in the first place.

Ask God to help you overcome your doubts and fears instead of dictating to him how you want your life to be.

> *"The thing that you do is not good. Both you and these people who are with you will surely wear yourselves out. For this thing is too much for you; you are not able to perform it by yourself."*
>
> —EX. 18:17–18

Moses is called by God to go back to Egypt to free God's people. We see repeatedly throughout the confrontations with the new pharaoh the insecurities in Moses, who continues to question God's judgment. Moses cannot get the message that God has everything under control and keeps trying to take it back himself.

Today's text occurs after the exodus from Egypt. People are having disputes and Moses is called upon to resolve them. The influence of his foster family is evident again when he attempts to control everything much like the pharaoh. Fortunately God provided Moses with a very wise father-in-law. Jethro recommended that Moses learn to delegate responsibility to appointed leaders.

Again we see another trait of work addiction—the belief that one is responsible for everything. Also notice how quickly Moses covered up the fear and anger he had displayed prior to the exodus.

Father, forgive my feeble efforts to try to control things that are too large for me to handle.

Then the LORD spoke to Moses and Aaron,
"Because you did not believe Me, to hallow Me in
the eyes of the children of Israel, therefore you shall
not bring this congregation into the land which I
have given them."
—NUM. 20:12

During his leadership in the wilderness, Moses developed a deep faith in God. He was able to allow God to be the one to discipline the disobedient tribes of Israel when previously he might have been tempted to take matters into his own hands.

In today's story, however, we see a return of anger and control issues. Instead of following God's exact command Moses speaks angrily to the people and strikes the rock instead of speaking to it. In addition he takes credit for the results instead of giving them to God. Consequently Moses was not permitted to go into the promised land.

So was Moses a workaholic? Certainly early in his life he demonstrated many of the symptoms. But in spite of Moses' background God used him as his vehicle to perform many miracles. Through God's work, Moses was converted from an angry man to a miraculous leader who had a humble faith in God and accepted responsibility.

In your recovery try not to get caught up in your lack of progress because God will prevail to finish the job.

> *Therefore gird up the loins of your mind, be sober,*
> *and rest your hope fully upon the grace that is to*
> *be brought to you at the revelation of Jesus Christ.*
> —1 PETER 1:13

Tim, a responsible professional, was becoming more anxious about failure in spite of his many accomplishments. His wife had put up with these tensions over the years but now she was aware of her codependency and was trying to change.

This only exacerbated Tim's tension because she wasn't there to pamper his pain. Finally she delivered an ultimatum for him to get some counseling.

His evaluation revealed a strong history of alcohol problems in his extended family. He was the oldest and had to fill in the gaps of irresponsibility left by his parents.

At work he was competent at whatever he did, but as his responsibilities increased so did his problems. In his current position his performance was excellent, but he was doing the work of three people. He admitted having a lack of trust in his other managers and an inability to delegate.

Eventually Tim was able to face his fears and discuss his problems with his superior.

Lord, I trust your authority in my life even when I must make changes at the office that are uncomfortable.

Not forsaking the assembling of ourselves together,
as is the manner of some, but exhorting one
another, and so much the more as you see the
Day approaching.   —HEB. 10:25

Do you think it would be a good idea for me to do something like that?" Donnie had heard that an alcoholic had made up a business card that said, *"I am a recovering alcoholic. Please do not offer me a drink."* Donnie was a workaholic/spendaholic who knew he had been out of control. He was looking for safeguards to protect him from falling back into his old patterns. He was opening himself up to accountability, a clear sign the denial was under control.

Donnie didn't realize it at the time, but he was practicing the twelfth step of the Twelve Step program: "Having had a spiritual awakening as a result of these steps, we tried to carry this message to ——aholics, and to practice these principles in all our affairs."

Recovery is never as effective when the person recovers alone. Two burning logs will keep the fire going; set one off by itself and the fire will go out. So it is with people. We workaholics keep our work and emotions in check more effectively when we are around others who know where we are. God has called us to a life of community. He wants to exhort us daily so that we might encourage others.

Two are better than one—their labor is more rewarding!

"For with God nothing will be impossible."
—LUKE 1:37

Lynn was a mess. She had just attempted suicide and failed. Now there were all the uncomfortable questions to answer, and she felt no one understood.

She realized the first step in dealing with her painful past was to recognize her helplessness. But her inability to control the perfectionism she had used to numb the pain drove her to despair.

She had refused to believe that there was anything or anyone who could make her whole again. So she was so convinced of that idea that she tried to end her own life.

She had actually been so comfortable with her pain that the thought of wholeness was too frightening to her. She rationalized that since there was not any hope, life was no longer worth enduring.

She felt that she could do nothing. She could not believe that through the person of Jesus Christ, God would bear fruit through her. Slowly she and I began an assault on that belief.

What do you believe God is able to do for you?

*But above all these things put on love, which is the
bond of perfection.*
—COL. 3:14

As a boy one of my favorite comic book superheroes
was Plastic Man. He wasn't as popular as some of the
other superheroes, but I was intrigued by some of the
things he did. His unique power was the ability to
adapt and stretch his body to meet the needs of the
situation. He could stretch his arm like a bullrope to
trip people, tie his arms in knots around villains, or
stretch across a ravine and be a human bridge for
others. No matter how many times he did this he still
was able to maintain his identity.

Although we can't do all these things, we can become more flexible. Workaholics often expect others
to adhere to their strict schedules without consideration of their needs. Sometimes we become irritated at
those who need our help or ask for a few hours of our
time.

*Although being organized is an important part of our lives, be con-
siderate of the needs of others. Also learn to be flexible when the
unexpected comes up.*

> *"And God will wipe away every tear from their eyes; there shall be no more death, nor sorrow, nor crying; and there shall be no more pain, for the former things have passed away."* —REV. 21:4

Anesthetics are a wonderful addition to medicine; we no longer have to "bite the bullet" as the cowboys of old did. I remember the time I had surgery and the doctor gave me a shot before wheeling me to the operating room. I felt so good that the surgeon could have said he was going to cut off my leg and I would not have minded!

The primary reason for addictive behaviors is to anesthetize pain. Consider Stan's case for a moment. Stan is a workaholic in the sense that he needed to escape to his work as a manager. One time his daughter was having surgery. Though his wife begged him to stay with her in the waiting room, he was drawn to the company like a moth to a light. He had to use his work to find relief.

The purpose of an anesthetic is to alleviate pain. It must never be confused with the task of removing pain, however. God has called us to face our pain bravely. In return, he promises to bring the healing we need.

———————————

The best anesthetic is the relief God provides.

*It is appointed for men to die once, but after this
the judgment.*
—HEB. 9:27

Schlitz Beer said it first: "You only go around once in
life, so go for all the gusto you can get." Not only does it
sound good, but it even agrees with the first half of the
verse from Hebrews. We do, indeed, live only one life
because the Scripture indicates we die only once.

But the beer slogan adds a principle that is usually
quite costly. To "go for all you can get" means that
someone has to pay a price for my bent toward self-
gratification. Today's verse, on the other hand, indicates just the opposite. I am responsible for what I do
or neglect, so totally that there will come a time of
judgment of my life. I cannot get all the gusto I want
without having to pay a price.

*What is it you are going for? Is it worth the price you will have to pay
some day?*

March 30 – ABSENT FATHERS

> *Blessed is he whose transgression is forgiven,*
> *Whose sin is covered.*
> —PS. 32:1

The phenomenon of absent workaholic fathers has become commonplace in our society. The workaholic's family members confess that family life does center around him. They try not to shatter his fragile reality by doing such unproductive things as play, make noise, or have fun.

The daughter of a workaholic explained that much of her daily life was dependent on the type of day her father had. His mood governed their behavior as a family. As a result, everyone else's needs and feelings were denied. This set the stage for the next generation of codependency.

Father, I confess that my addiction has left many victims in my own family. Forgive me and help others to forgive me so I can reconcile the damage.

> *The words of the wise are like goads, and the*
> *words of scholars are like well-driven nails, given*
> *by one Shepherd.*   —ECCL. 12:11

Vince Lombardi is one of the greatest football coaches of all times. His antics are legendary. At times Lombardi would supposedly attack his players physically if they were not performing to potential. He had his players' respect because they knew that he was there for them. He drew their best from them and made them winners.

One of the keys to maturation is our willingness to take criticism constructively. If we are dedicated to pursuing truth and willing to live honestly we must change our thinking about criticism. Solomon recognized that words of wisdom were like goads, sharp sticks the farmers used to motivate their mules. The words that we need to hear are often painful. We may kick against the goads instinctively, but if we realize that we are being nudged in the right direction we should respond properly and thankfully.

Solomon also said that words of wisdom were tent-stakes. He presents the anchoring, securing element to the imparting and receiving of wisdom. What a helpful picture he presents!

Lord, help us to realize your goads and tentstakes are all good for us.

> *And the LORD God said, "It is not good that man*
> *should be alone; I will make him a helper*
> *comparable to him."* —GEN. 2:18

Janice was an excellent lawyer. She had impressive credentials and a great track record. The problem was that she practiced law in her marriage as well as in the courtroom.

To be good a lawyer needs to accomplish three things. First, she can leave no stone uncovered in preparation for her case. Second, she must present her case convincingly. Third, she must reveal the flaws and absurdities in her opponent's presentation.

She was a lawyer to the core and could not turn it off. Her husband, Peter, was gifted, accomplished, educated, and genuine. He truly loved her, but he could never please her. Either what he did was not good enough, or he would do well in one area but then hear about his failure in a different area.

It is impossible to please the perfectionist. The "lawyer perfectionist" is harder still because she leaves no room for any other perspective. Janice first had to learn to recognize her own unrealistic standards for Peter. The more she demanded, the more he was driven away and the lonelier she became.

Are you contributing to your own loneliness?

And Adam said:
"This is now bone of my bones
And flesh of my flesh;
She shall be called Woman,
Because she was taken out of Man."
—GEN. 2:23

The perfectionist mindset is adept at criticism. The flaws Janice saw in Peter were accurate, so she was left in a double bind. How could she accept him, with full knowledge that he was not totally adequate?

The Scriptures give an interesting answer to this dilemma which confronts marriages where at least one partner is obsessive. Today's verse usually is quoted or referenced with emphasis on the "taken out of Man" phrase. But in the larger context, Adam is essentially saying, "I accept this person. I take her as she is. I acknowledge her roots."

How could he accept her? Think about it. What did he know about her? Nothing. The Scriptures indicate that not a single word passed between the two of them before he said this passage. He knew nothing of her preferences, desires, or abilities.

The *only* thing he knew about Eve was who brought her to him. And solely on the basis of God's stated faithfulness to him, Adam accepted Eve, because he knew God was committed to meeting his needs, regardless of how Eve performed.

Are you able to look beyond your mate, depend on God, and accept the partner you have, complete with faults?

> *The LORD is good,*
> *A stronghold in the day of trouble;*
> *And He knows those who trust in Him.*
> —NAH. 1:7

Doubt is a big hurdle for a workaholic. Mary was beginning to realize this.

As the oldest in her family Mary had often sought approval by caring for younger siblings. Then she married Ed, who seemed sensitive, understanding, and not very demanding. She was completely disillusioned early in the marriage about all these things. Ed didn't initiate much, so she just pitched in as always to maintain the home and children.

As she slowed down her doubts creeped in. She feared that if she slacked off her marriage and family would fall apart and Ed might leave her. As a Christian she even began to doubt her own salvation.

Eventually Mary learned to trust God and communicate her fears to her family. Most important, she learned that her salvation was intact the day she became a Christian and that God wanted to relieve her of her need to trade work for love.

Lord, I confess to you my doubts that at times include my salvation. Lift the burden of oppressive thoughts that keep me from letting myself go into your loving arms.

"For My yoke is easy and My burden is light."
—MATT. 11:30

High school gyms are always a hotbed of activity. I arrived at the high school gym one evening after my daughter's volleyball practice. While I waited for her I read the bulletin board. A sign, strategically placed by a coach, caught my eye. It said, "You must give 110 percent in order to gain 100 percent." Sounds impressive, does it not? The problem for me is that it does not make any sense. It would be similar to spending $110 to make $100; the government may operate that way, but it has never worked for me.

This quote sheds light on a problem that my daughter and I share: we try too hard to succeed. On the racquetball court I will get uptight from trying too hard, and my timing and patience get thrown off. I see it happen to golfers regularly.

This slogan represents another one of those messages that tell us that we must be driven. It is important that we challenge such thinking. God does. Someone once said that if you give to God, the remaining percentage will go further than the 100 percent if you kept it. The same can be said of our emotional and physiological resources.

Little is much when God is in it.

> *But Jesus said, "Let the little children come to Me,*
> *and do not forbid them; for of such is the kingdom*
> *of heaven."*   —MATT. 19:14

We often refer to one part of recovery as reparenting. It usually comes after grieving the loss of the ideal past we never had. It hurts to know we can't get a refund on lost time. There is conciliation, however, in the knowledge that our Lord understands this hurt. I have found it helpful to conceptualize reparenting by differentiating myself functionally. One part of me is independent, responsible, adequate, rational, and confident. I refer to this part as the Man (or Woman). The other part of me is dependent, irresponsible, inadequate, and moody. I refer to this part affectionately as the Little Boy (or Girl). As I conceptualize it the Man's primary responsibility is to care for the needs of the Little Boy. To me an ideal parent meets the dependency needs of the child but also equips the child to meet those needs alone.

Unfortunately most workaholics never were Little Boys or Girls. They deny their dependency needs and fail to realize that those needs exist throughout life.

Since we can't get a refund on the past, only God can reparent us.

At that time the disciples came to Jesus, saying,
"Who then is greatest in the kingdom of heaven?"
. . . "Whoever humbles himself as this little child is
the greatest in the kingdom of heaven."
—MATT. 18:1, 4

Today's text picks up where we left off yesterday in our discussion of reparenting. We described the ideal scenario if one had had ideal parents. A fully integrated adult would be someone who had an internal Man or Woman who was able to take care of the Little Boy or Girl.

In questioning Christ, the disciples logically approached him from their Man and asked him to give them the ground rules to get into heaven. I can imagine how confused they were when he suggested they must receive him as children do. The thought of being Little Boys again was the last thing they expected.

The good news of the gospel is that through Christ's death, we are given permission to be Little Boys and Girls again. Our heavenly Father promises to meet the needs of that child no matter what our experience was growing up. He equips us with the Holy Spirit to empower our Man or Woman to do what he has given us to do.

_____

With the heart of a child I talk to Christ and with the power of the Holy Spirit I walk with Christ as a Man.

> *At that time Jesus answered and said, "I thank*
> *You, Father, Lord of heaven and earth, because You*
> *have hidden these things from the wise and prudent*
> *and have revealed them to babes. Even so, Father,*
> *for so it seemed good in Your sight."*
> —MATT. 11:25–26

The whole notion of being reparented by God is totally illogical to active workaholics. But to those who are past their denial and have lost all hope, the words of Christ are like a breath of fresh air. God is pleased when we come to him as children.

Many Christians get confused here, because Paul later says in Scripture that we are to give up childish ways. The difference is that Paul is referring to behavior, whereas Christ is referring to the language of the heart.

This language is the logic of the emotions which is dependent, helpless, selfish, and inadequate. On the positive side the child is creative, fun loving, and affectionate.

I believe God is saying he wants to be there to respond to all of our needs. We can then behave appropriately because we truly want to please and be close to our Father.

God, I do want to be your child as you describe so many times in your Word. You can restore me to be the Man or Woman you made me to be.

Now the body is . . . for the Lord, and the Lord for the body.
—1 COR. 6:13

One of the most popular songs of the sixties was "I'll Never Fall in Love Again," by Dionne Warwicke. She sings, "What do you get when you fall in love?" Now answer this question: "What do you get when you overwork?" You get enough . . .

- job dissatisfaction
- lowered self-confidence and esteem
- increased job tension
- deterioration of interpersonal relationships
- lower creative input
- decrease in decision-making quality
- apathy, cynicism, and pessimism

. . . . to get depressed.

Why do we do it? There are many reasons: guilt, misinformation, identity, money, and the list goes on. Regardless of the reasons we must stop for a moment and remember today's verse. As we realize that our bodies are the temple of the Holy Spirit we will understand that God is very concerned about its upkeep. In the Old Testament he went to great pains to spell out the construction and care for the tabernacle. He cares even more about us.

Lord, please rule in us and help us to be good custodians.

April 9 – THE RIGHT STUFF

> *Thus says the LORD:*
> *"Let not the wise man glory in his wisdom,*
> *Let not the mighty man glory in his might,*
> *Nor let the rich man glory in his riches."*
> —JER. 9:23

On a call-in public-radio program, the guest host was the director of a sleep disorder clinic. He was fielding questions from people with sleep problems. One call was from the wife of a medical intern who noticed his behavior and attitude worsened whenever he went without sleep. She asked why the medical community forces its interns to work far beyond healthy endurance. The doctor said that the medical community takes a "let's-see-what-kind-of-man-you-are" approach. The result is that both intern and patient suffer.

Doctors are not the only group pressured into drivenness. The attitude is part of the underlying fabric of our society. Driven people claim that you cannot accomplish much of importance if you do not possess the "right stuff." It's good to know that God calls us to a perspective that is quite different. This verse tells us that "bragging rights" are based solely on our understanding of God and his ways.

The break you take to meditate might be the best work you do today!

*"I have glorified You on the earth. I have finished
the work which You have given Me to do."*
—JOHN 17:4

The workaholic's work is never done. The need to accomplish demands that more work be done better, faster, or cheaper. But above all the work must be done.

Was Jesus a workaholic? The verse in John 17 records that he completed the work God the Father had given him to do. Since he had accomplished the whole job, it would seem that he at least *could* have been obsessive.

But were all the sick healed? Was everyone restored spiritually? Had every injustice been righted? If not, then how could he say he had completed his work?

To say that any of the above arguments determined whether or not Jesus finished his task is to use the wrong scale. Because of his priorities, it was possible for him to have finished when so much was left to be done.

What standard do you use to measure whether or not you have finished a task or assignment? Do you know whether or not it is the right ruler?

Son of God, help me to measure my accomplishments by the same standards of performance that you use for my life.

> *"Is this not the word that we told you in Egypt, saying, 'Let us alone that we may serve the Egyptians?' For it would have been better for us to serve the Egyptians than that we should die in the wilderness."*
>
> —EX. 14:12

One of Aesop's fables has an important message. A wolf is envious of a dog who has shelter and food provided daily by his master. The dog is willing to change places with the wolf. However, when the wolf discovers the purpose for the collar and chain attached to the dog, he realizes the cost for easy living is too great and wisely moves on. Slavery is too high a price for easy living.

The setting for today's verse is the shores of the Red Sea. The Israelites are standing with their backs to it, facing the oncoming Egyptians. They had left the life of slavery to the Egyptians for the promised land, but had not anticipated that freedom would be costly. They longed for the life of the dog, trading slavery for safety.

Are you miserable in your work but stay for the benefits? Do you escape to the slavery of work to avoid the pain of difficult family and personal life?

Slavery is too high a price for easy living.

Do not love the world or the things in the world. If anyone loves the world, the love of the Father is not in him.
                                        —1 JOHN 2:15

As our recovery progresses we must continue to expand our awareness of the many ways our addiction to work is intertwined with our environment. We would now like to take several days to focus on the organizations in which we work.

When we recover from a work addiction we often make the mistake of assuming that the problem is only in us. Nothing could be so untrue. Codependency is so prevalent in our society that the workplace is not immune.

We will look at several characteristics in the workplace this week that will help you in your efforts to recover. To assist in this process we will consult Anne Wilson Schaef and Diane Fassell's work, *Addictive Organization*. In this book they analyze how these organizations communicate, think, manage their personnel, and how they appear in structure.

Practice looking at your office through a different lens. Give thought to how individuals operate on the basis of principles and goals versus being driven and going through the motions.

> *For all that is in the world . . . is not of the Father*
> *but is of the world.* —1 JOHN 2:16

Part of our addiction to work can be tied to life in the organization itself. One thing we have to guard against is the promises the organization makes.

The problem for the workaholic in recovery is that he or she is working hard enough now. Promises feed into this process through a future versus a "here-and-now" orientation. These promises can take the form of advancement and financial comfort or they can be part of a larger cause or mission.

These promises make workaholics particularly vulnerable in that they seem to offer a second chance at something they perhaps didn't have growing up—the promise of acceptance and love without a price.

We need to realize that we must always pay a price for any promise. In addictive organizations the price one usually pays is the same price one paid as a child. This is the same process that occurred in our codependent families where control overrode one's needs or feelings.

_____

Father, help me to recognize what are legitimate promises and what are promises to entice me into my addictive patterns.

Where there is no wood, the fire goes out;
And where there is no talebearer, strife ceases.
—PROV. 26:20

Organizations that contribute to workaholism have certain styles by which they communicate. Schaef and Fassel list several of these characteristics. First, the communication is *indirect*. When communication is indirect people feel they are unable to discuss conflicts that occur and tend to avoid them.

Another characteristic is a high level of *gossip and secrets*. When people can't get information directly they resort to gossip. This results in inaccurate information and affects the quality of the work that is done. With secrets, the information can be accurate but because it is shared inappropriately it causes unnecessary tensions between groups or coalitions that can impede the work.

Finally, addictive organizations do not allow for *expression of feelings*. Those who do risk sharing feelings are often criticized and may even lose their jobs.

These characteristics are identical to those symptoms seen in codependent families. If you are to maintain your recovery it is imperative you consider these aspects of your work environment.

―――――――

Does your workplace communicate clearly and effectively so you know what is expected and how you are doing?

In all labor there is profit,
But idle chatter leads only to poverty.
—PROV. 14:23

Addictive organizations also have characteristic ways of thinking as Schaef and Fassel have identified. The first of these is *loss of corporate memory or forgetfulness*. Often the organization takes on too much work as if unaware of the work it already has.

Another quality of thinking in these companies is *externalization*. The organization acts as if it is acceptable for people to bring their personal issues into the workplace. Typically this will happen when addicted individuals are in key positions in the organization. These people act out and force others to put up with it for fear of losing their job.

Finally, a quality of *dualism* operates in addictive organizations. Dualism tends to view the workplace as black and white. If a new idea is seen as coming from the enemy camp, it is not accepted. Consequently the organization is stuck when decisions must be made.

Does your organization take on more work than it should without concern for the employees? Does it fail to learn from past mistakes?

He who keeps instruction is in the way of life,
But he who refuses reproof goes astray.
                                        —PROV. 10:17

A final process we need to be conscious of in our recovery efforts is management styles. Schaef and Fassel list several in this area which you may wish to read about in more detail. These include denial, isolation, self-centeredness, and judgmentalism.

Denial operates when decisions are made without considering what is going on internally with workers or without considering how the customer or consumer views what you do.

Isolation and Self-centeredness are both related to denial in that they tend to withdraw from the marketplace or see themselves as the "center of the universe."

Judgmentalism tends to evaluate the work of others as either good or bad without considering them as people with strengths and weaknesses. It tends to cramp creativity and fosters fear and paranoia.

Does your organization treat people as people? If not, these styles may contribute to your addiction.

> *The Gentiles shall see your righteousness,*
> *And all kings your glory.*
> *You shall be called by a new name,*
> *Which the mouth of the LORD will name.*
> —ISA. 62:2

A psychologist named Garmazy devoted his research to the study of the "invulnerable child," one who grows up to be a productive member of society against all odds. She may have been inner city, orphaned or neglected, with little or no environmental support. Garmazy found that the common denominator among these children was that they found a mentor—an adult who modeled values and stability to them.

There will always be more opportunities to do wrong than to do right. If eternal vigilance is the price of liberty, then I suppose it is true of integrity as well. In this society of options we must stay on the course toward the important things—the things that will lead us through a fulfilling life and provide the greatest service to others. Jesus did. Mother Teresa is doing it. Although we may never sacrifice as extensively as they did, our children are counting on us to pave the way. Is there a child in your life who is looking at you and learning integrity?

Lord, help us never to forget that little eyes are watching us—even those that do not belong to our own children.

Indeed, we put bits in horses' mouths that they may obey us, and we turn their whole body.
—JAMES 3:3

When I was ten my grandfather taught me how to ride a horse. He had made his livelihood by breaking horses, so he knew what to do. I first learned that the horse wants to know one thing: who is in control here?

After some preliminaries, Gramps taught me how to ride Paint, a horse who liked to have his own way.

The New Mexico sky was pale blue that day, and I can still remember what Gramps said. "Son, this horse is going to run away with you. He thinks he's stronger than you are. Just let him run and hang on. Then, when he starts to slow down because he's getting tired, you whip him and make him keep running. You've got to show him that it will cost him when he tries to take control from you."

Paint ran. I held on. When he started to slow down I would not let him. And Gramps was right. I learned to ride that day, and Paint never ran on me again.

Workaholics need control. It usually costs them, just as it cost Paint that day.

———————

Are there relationships or situations where you are fighting for control that does not belong to you?

April 19 – LAUGHTER AS THERAPY

> *Go, eat your bread with joy,*
> *And drink your wine with a merry heart;*
> *For God has already accepted your works.*
> —ECCL. 9:7

The roar of laughter from the lunchroom wafted into the reception area of our clinic. It was enough to bring an emissary from the Serious World back to investigate what was going on. This was not just laughter, but hysterical laughter that rarely comes your way. It was the type of laughter that breeds laughter itself, making irrelevant the original reason for the laugh. We laughed at each other laughing.

The counseling profession is a sobering one. It is stressful work and the burnout rate is high. We needed to come apart so we would not come apart.

The emissary from the Serious World understood what was going on. She knew better than to say, "Keep it down. There are serious people out here." At other times I would be in a counseling session and hear the same roar from the lunchroom. I would pause, listen, and vicariously enjoy the laugh until it ebbed, realizing it was therapy itself.

Enjoy your work with a merry heart today. Have a good laugh.

————————

Lord, thank you for the gift of laughter. Help us to make full use of it.

*If anyone competes in athletics, he is not crowned
unless he competes according to the rules.*
—2 TIM. 2:5

Phillip was a runner. Twice he had participated in the
Marine Corps Marathon and finished in the top third.
He was not fanatic about running, but he followed a
training schedule consistently. He was a good long-
distance man.

But that only applied to his running. He treated
every other area of his life as though it were a one-
hundred-yard dash. He worked more than sixty hours
per week and rarely slept more than four hours a
night. He seldom took time to eat lunch.

I met him when he was in his twenties. He was mys-
tified because he could not figure out why he was already burning out. He was running out of control
everywhere except on the racetrack. He had the discipline to pace himself for twenty-six miles, but he could
not apply the same principle to his life.

Eventually he began to listen to others and then he
began to pace his life.

Is someone trying to tell you to slow down? Could
they possibly see something about you that you cannot
see?

―――――――――

Lord, help me listen to you and to those you have put in my life.

April 21 – THE POWER OF EXAMPLE

*You shall teach them diligently to your children,
and shall talk of them when you sit in your house,
when you walk by the way, when you lie down, and
when you rise up.* —DEUT. 6:7

The late evangelist Bill Rice valued his time with his family. He spent a lot of time away from home and was deprived of the opportunity to play with his boys. One day he was romping around the house as a horse and the boys were riding him horseback. Some visitors came by to conduct church business. Rather than stopping and gaining his professional composure, he continued with the horseplay, inviting the guests to make themselves comfortable until he was finished. What an impact that must have made on his sons!

The examples that we set by our actions are far more powerful than the things we say. We have counseled many adult children of workaholics who are bitter and mistrustful because they have been betrayed by their caregivers. Scripture admonishes us in this verse to teach our children well with the implication that we must spend time with them. Do not let anything get in the way.

Lord, help us to set a guard on our family jewels and protect them.

A time to break down,
And a time to build up.
—ECCL. 3:3

I often tune in to "This Old House" on PBS. I watch craftsmen transform a doomed building into a work of art better than the original. I have always been impressed by their effort to preserve the building's original identity, however. The old trim, doors, and flooring remain. The beautiful aspects are painstakingly refurbished. The craftsmen treat their work with the love and commitment reminiscent of an Old World guild.

As in all TV there is also great illusion. An immense amount of work—the tearing down of walls, the replacement of roofs, the digging of foundations—is accomplished behind the scenes. And there is never any mess to clean up.

How like our lives. We were not only dilapidated, we were condemned. But God sees the potential and has begun his good work. There is much to tear down, there is much to clean up—and we don't have the luxury of a fade button.

Dear God, may we trust you as you apply your skills to our frame. Help us to endure the pain of tearing down and the drudgery of cleaning up.

> *"They also took some of the fruit of the land in their hands and brought it down to us; and they brought back word to us, saying, 'It is a good land which the LORD our God is giving us.' Nevertheless you would not go up, but rebelled."*
>
> —DEUT. 1:25–26

Whenever a space launch lifts from Cape Canaveral the astronauts know there is a period in which they can still abort the mission if necessary. After that there is no turning back. The same application can be made to other major decisions in life. After a point we must either commit to move on regardless of the risk or abort, turn back, and resist change.

Such is the story behind today's verse. The children of Israel had the opportunity to enter the promised land after their dry journey through the desert. They looked past God's promise of victory and feared their circumstances instead. They aborted the mission and had to spend the next forty years wandering the desert as a result.

The result of facing crises and taking risks is growth. To resist change, on the other hand, will *always* result in stagnation.

———————

Lord, help us to face our points of no return with courage.

"There is no one who has left house . . . for My sake . . . who shall not receive a hundredfold."
—MARK 10:29–30

Another aspect of recovery is the notion of leaving home. This is part of the grieving process in which we emotionally transfer dependency from parents to ourselves. Many of us assume this automatically happens when we are adults, but in actuality it tends to be a lifelong process. Workaholics often have a compounded problem because they come from homes devoid of unconditional love.

Because getting love often had strings attached in childhood, those strings become ropes by adulthood which bind us to a life of performance. In order to leave home properly we must first follow these strings back to their source and disconnect from the old themes. This quite often leads to grieving as we choose to relinquish the old controls.

At this point, through our renewed attachment to Christ, we are able to learn how to love and be loved unconditionally.

Lord, I do wish to follow your command to leave father and mother, but I need your guidance to trace the distorted strings of my attachment.

> *The man answered and said to them, "Why, this is*
> *a marvelous thing, that you do not know where He*
> *is from, and yet He has opened my eyes!"*
> —JOHN 9:30

Diana was obsessed with not rocking the boat at home and keeping husband and children happy. She worked a difficult and demanding full-time job so they could afford their mortgage. She avoided conflicts and arguments for the sake of keeping peace at all costs. In order to keep her husband happy, she set no sexual limitations, so he was free to do and demand anything.

But Diana was blind. She wanted peace so much she could not see what was happening to her and her family. She was quickly becoming worn out and used up. Her husband was becoming completely self-centered and selfish. Her children were learning a distorted way of living that would follow them into their adulthood.

But Diana began to see. She first had a renewed encounter with the Savior who can open blind eyes. Because he could see, the blind man in John 9 did not avoid conflict with the religious leaders who held considerable power over him. The next step for Diana was to stop avoiding conflict.

Are you blindly avoiding conflict with someone or something?

*Therefore, putting away lying, each one speak truth
with his neighbor, for we are members of one
another.*
                                                —EPH. 4:25

Once Diana saw the destruction taking place in her
family she was ready to begin speaking the truth. The
problem was she did not know how to do so. Her pattern of denial of self was so habitual that she had difficulty recognizing the validity of her perspective on
things.

To overturn that habit she had to find out what was
true for her and then say it. Her silence had actually
been a form of lying. When she avoided conflict by not
speaking what was true to her about the abuses taking
place in their home she was lying.

She began to speak the truth by setting limits. When
she began to say no, conflicts resulted. Her husband
did not like hearing the truth about his selfishness. Her
children did not like having to be responsible for things
Mom had always done before.

Though it happened over time, the result of her setting limits was that she and her family became
healthier. She had spoken the truth by setting limits.

God in heaven, enable me to see and speak the truth correctly.

> *"These are the things you shall do:*
> *Speak each man the truth to his neighbor;*
> *Give judgment in your gates for truth, justice,*
> *   and peace."*
> —ZECH. 8:16

When Diana began to speak the truth and to set limits with her husband and children, more was affected than just her present life. She realized she had not been speaking the truth to herself about her past.

She had been abused as a child and had lied to herself about it. The lies looked so reasonable. "It was my fault," she had said. "I really deserved it." When she said, "They did the best they could," she came closest to the truth.

Telling herself the truth was more painful than telling her husband the truth. When she spoke the truth to herself about her abuse, only then could she grieve what she had lost.

Grieving hurts; it did for Diana. But much to her surprise, the pain of grieving was followed by the freedom of knowing the truth. She found that spoken truth hurts much less than unresolved grief.

Speaking the truth is rarely easy or automatic. If it were then there would be no need for the Scriptures to command us to do so.

Are you telling yourself and those in your life the truth?

Therefore my heart is glad, and my glory rejoices;
My flesh also will rest in hope.
For You will not leave my soul. —PS. 16:9–10

Work as an addiction is very easy to deny because it doesn't seem to have the obvious problems of addiction. However, we are learning this may no longer be true.

There now seem to be growing bodies of evidence that would suggest that workaholics may in fact be drug addicted. The drug in this case is not taken by mouth but is already built in. The name of the drug is *adrenaline.*

Why might this be considered drug abuse? To understand this we must understand how the adrenal system works. Adrenaline helps us react in situations where we are in danger or need to be more assertive to accomplish a task. It gives the body that extra boost it needs to run from danger or to finish our work.

When the body must prepare constantly for a task an overload can occur. The result is the adrenal system doesn't know when to shut down because rest times are too sporadic or inconsistent.

Do you feel most alive when you are dealing with a crisis? You may be addicted to adrenaline. Rest today!

*Because the sentence against an evil work is not
executed speedily, therefore the heart of the sons of
men is fully set in them to do evil.*

—ECCL. 8:11

In some Middle Eastern countries crime is punished
swiftly, severely, and decisively. The result is that the
crime rates are very low for these countries. (That is
not to say I endorse such extreme measures; there is
little built-in protection for error.) On the other hand,
our crime rate is outrageous. Criminals have found that
sentences may not be carried out for years and that
their time is often shortened. They soon laugh at the
system and carry on.

Solomon makes a point in this verse that because
justice is not harsh and swift we will tend to think we
are all right. What we may forget is the long-term con-
sequence of our actions. Some of the most bitter, miserable, and callous people I have met are those who
look back over their lives with regret, focusing on the
missed opportunities and feeling helpless and hopeless
as their dreams fade away. They failed to commit to
integrity and balance early on in life, and they did not
have enough to carry them through the difficult times.

Reevaluate what is important to you now while there
is still time.

_____

Lord, help us not to take advantage of your grace and longsuffering.

All things are lawful for me, but all things are
not helpful.   —1 COR. 10:23

In our recovery we need to learn about the variety of addictive agents and behaviors that keep us locked into our addictive lifestyle. Some of these items include not only drugs and alcohol, but also caffeine, sugar, or salt.

Christians are particularly vulnerable to trying to proselyte others about the sins of their old addiction. This behavior can be addictive itself, as they try to control everyone else. They are usually more effective when they quietly try to change their behavior without trying to draw attention to their program.

Often giving up work transfers into an addiction to rage. This occurs when the feelings begin to thaw out and addicts justify their intense feelings as part of recovery. Usually if they exercise some self-control without shutting off the feelings they will discover pain is there. Pain is a much more hospitable emotion to communicate.

Father, through your Spirit help me not to let anything rule my life but you.

What then shall we say to these things? If God is for us, who can be against us? —ROM. 8:31

One characteristic of workaholism is the belief that you cannot depend on anyone for support. There are a number of reasons for this self-sufficiency. You may have been raised to not trust. You may feel inadequate: to seek help would exacerbate feelings of weakness and vulnerability. Guilt can be a determining factor: you do not want to inconvenience others. Whatever the reasons, total self-reliance is unhealthy. Your circuits will overload and you will become isolated.

In today's verse, Paul was commenting on all of the things that God had to do to provide eternal life for us. He ended his thought with this exclamation: "If God is for us who can be against us?" The answer, of course, is no one. The Lord has gone through a great deal of trouble to protect and provide for us. We need to let down some of the barriers we have constructed to keep others at a safe distance. We do not need to prove our strength to anyone. God is for us.

Dear Lord, thank you for being for me. Help me to remember that when I am not even for myself.

So He Himself often withdrew into the wilderness and prayed.
—LUKE 5:16

We have gone from "Early to bed, early to rise, makes a man healthy, wealthy, and wise" to "Late to bed, early to rise, leads me to addiction, affliction, and demise."

I like to look to Christ as my model for the work ethic. To me he seems to exemplify the perfect balance of work and rest. When he worked he worked hard, but he spent large amounts of time with his disciples and with God the Father.

Workaholics do not permit themselves to waste time. Labor-saving devices such as car phones, dicta-phones, and laptop computers do wonders to save time. To an addict, however, they simply become the tools to get more work in over the same long workday.

If I am ever to recover from my addiction to work I must be willing to give up time to doing absolutely nothing in order to give my body and mind time to recuperate.

———

Father, help me to let go of my need to control my time. Give me a proper perspective on what you consider idle time; help me to remember that your Son Christ frequently rested before his next day of work.

> *I acknowledged my sin to You,*
> *And my iniquity I have not hidden.*
> *I said, "I will confess my transgressions to the LORD,"*
> *And You forgave the iniquity of my sin.*
>
> —PS. 32:5

Sorry is a deceiving word, because it allows us to admit guilt without actually having to change. To say "I'm sorry" might only mean "I'm sorry you feel that way," excluding any remorse. Addicts are famous for false repentances.

Repentance begins with humility. Change must begin inside us—it can never be forced or cajoled out of us. God has determined never to invade our will. Think about that for a moment. He wants us to exercise our will toward him, to give control over to him. We tend to not listen to such ideas. The stubbornness of our will causes us to keep doing things our way until we are literally at the end of our rope. As strange as it may sound, the person who is contemplating suicide may not be at the end of his rope, but at the end of his will.

The positive part of despair is the new opportunity to solve problems in a different way—God's way. Have you approached God with hat in hand, ready to face and admit your shortcomings? You may never find rest until you do.

No one has ever seen God while standing on her feet.

*We ourselves boast of you . . . for your patience
and faith in all your persecutions and tribulations.*
—2 THESS. 1:4

Workaholics have a way of using crisis as a means of taking the spotlight off their addiction. This characteristic is fueled by an illusion of control. Work addicts believe they have to be in control, so they move from crisis to crisis, with little time to rest in between. Most of these crises are over the simple things like mailing the bills or making a work decision. There are also frequent conflicts during these crises with blame being projected in many directions among family members.

It is not easy to break out of the crisis orientation. To do so we must change the way we think. If we can give up the need to control these things we can eliminate the number of crises in our lives. At first this may result in more conflict with others who are used to the old system, but they will adapt if we only respond to legitimate crises.

Father, teach me to trust in your providence and control over my life. Help me to respond only to crises that are real.

And He said to them, "Come aside by yourselves to a deserted place and rest a while." For there were many coming and going, and they did not even have time to eat.　　　　　—MARK 6:31

I cringed at the words of the chorale as they sang, "I would rather burn out for Jesus than rust out for the devil." Have you ever wondered what it means exactly to burn out? Burnout is really a process that seems to follow this pattern:

Stage One: physical/emotional exhaustion; inability to relax;

Stage Two: loss of concern for people and emotional responsiveness;

Stage Three: depression, self-depreciation, cynicism, and hopelessness.

I do not think that Jesus had this pattern in mind for us. He certainly did not model such patterns for us. He regulated and paced his life. He was prepared for difficult days and still maintained his care for people. He had to admonish his disciples in this passage to rest.

Be reminded—there is always more to do than you have time for. Conserve your strength; pace yourself.

Lord, help us to maintain ourselves so that we neither rust out nor burn out, for whatever the purpose.

"The heart is deceitful above all things,
And desperately wicked;
Who can know it?
I, the LORD, search the heart,
I test the mind."   —JER. 17:9–10

In her book *When Society Becomes An Addict*, Anne Wilson Schaef examines the dishonesty that exists in the workaholic. She identifies a form of language known as "the three ifs" that gets used to cover up the addiction.

The first of these is "if only." This phrase is an effort to duck responsibility for one's problem by fixing blame somewhere in the past. "If only I had not gotten into this mortgage I wouldn't have to work so hard." Statements like this prevent us from facing the past and seeing what our responsibility or feelings may have been.

The second if is "as if." Workaholics are usually out of touch with reality in the present. They act "as if" they are like everyone else or how they perceive others. Because they can never let others see the real person they live in constant fear of being found out and being rejected.

The third if is "what if." Addicts try to control the events of the future by asking "What if this?" or "What if that?" By doing this they avoid the present.

Lord, teach me to be accountable to you and others for my past.

> *And she brought forth her firstborn Son, and*
> *wrapped Him in swaddling cloths, and laid Him in*
> *a manger, because there was no room for them in*
> *the inn.*
> —LUKE 2:7

We all know this story, but did you ever stop to consider how this innkeeper missed it? The most important birth in history could have taken place in *his* hotel, but he missed it. Of course he must have been busy. I imagine that the guests were demanding and it was hard to keep supplies stocked. But he did not even see his most important guest.

Greg was like that. He attended to his career, his golf swing, and his tennis serve. But he was an innkeeper. He missed seeing his family.

He was at home enough. He seldom came home later than six o'clock and he did not travel much. He was with his family, but he was not there. He was shocked when his wife told him she could take it no more. She said he could start noticing her and the kids or they would leave. It was his choice.

He still has not chosen; however, in a way his indecision is a choice. He is still an innkeeper, missing those most important.

_____

Are you an innkeeper in your home? Are you giving your attention to who is most important?

*For by grace you have been saved through faith,
and that not of yourselves; it is the gift of God, not
of works, lest anyone should boast.*
—EPH. 2:8–9

Workaholics often talk about their accomplishments. At the core of this behavior is a strong need to be recognized and accepted. At first others may be impressed, but those who know them longer see them as selfish, self-centered, or insecure, all of which are true.

We must realize that accomplishments are meaningless when motivated by our insecurity. Work successes will not fill our emptiness and will only fuel false pride.

Our text for today is a perfect reminder of this. It points out that our wholeness is a gift from God. We didn't work it out on our own.

Most workaholics don't consider themselves as braggers. They may even verbally give God the credit, but only superficially.

Ask those closest to you for honest feedback if you have problems in this area, and ask them to hold you accountable.

Dear Lord, I confess I do bring too much focus on my accomplishments to get approved by others. Help me again to be satisfied with your gift of grace.

> *His flesh shall be young like a child's,*
> *He shall return to the days of his youth.*
> —JOB 33:25

I once visited the Lehigh Valley Railroad Museum in Sayre, Pennsylvania, where hobbyists have recreated a miniature of the local railroad system as it must have been fifty years ago. The scene is incredible. The curators painstakingly attended to every detail on the trains and the surrounding community. Obviously an immense amount of time and love went into this project.

The project was also a healthy release for the hobbyists' need for perfection. It is certainly a positive way to release tension, and there is nothing wrong with escaping stress by journeying to the past as it is remembered.

The men tending the museum trains all had a gleam in their eyes; a sense of accomplishment exuded from them. They had learned a lesson of life and they knew it. The real railyard is dead and gone. The town built around the railroad is barely alive. Yet these men, many of whom no doubt worked on the railroad, seemed more alive than ever.

Lord, thank you for memories and the ability to recreate them.

> *Then Philip went down to the city of Samaria and preached Christ to them. . . . Go toward the south along the road. . . . Go near and overtake this chariot.*
> —ACTS 8:5, 26, 29

This story of Philip in the book of Acts is most interesting. He starts out in a city in Samaria where many people are responding to his preaching. But then he receives instruction to leave that very productive setting and go to an empty desert road. There he is told to approach one particular chariot.

The man in the chariot takes Philip's message to his home in Ethiopia. History shows that a legitimate Christian influence has been in that country since the first century. It was a good thing that Philip followed the instruction. He was never given the big picture. He was never told that as productive as his time in a *city* was, this strange trip to a desert road would result in reaching a *nation*.

Most people who struggle with obsession and perfection think they have to see the whole picture. If they know they cannot complete a job in the time available they tend to not start it at all. If they cannot see the end result from the start they will not take the chance.

Lord, help me to be more like Philip. Help me take what I know and go with that, even though I cannot see the end from the beginning.

> *"Therefore do not worry about tomorrow, for tomorrow will worry about its own things. Sufficient for the day is its own trouble."*
> —MATT. 6:34

Ted struggled with excessive anxiety about the future. He was a successful manager at his company and had a good salary which included liberal retirement benefits. In spite of this he still insisted that he needed plenty of extra put aside for the unexpected.

His family members were glad he was working fewer hours now but were frustrated that money seemed to be his primary concern. One day his son accused him of caring more about his retirement than him. The light bulb went on as Ted recalled his father, a factory worker who always preached about saving for tomorrow. Ted never understood why the other kids' fathers who worked in the mills could afford to take them places.

Ted finally realized that he had been denying his father's alcohol abuse and his own anger about that. Ted saw that he was overcompensating for the future that never came as a child because his father drank it away.

Take an inventory of your family history, paying particular attention to people who perhaps had problems with work, gambling, or excessive anger.

Now Jephthah the Gileadite was a mighty man of valor, but he was the son of a harlot. . . . When his wife's sons grew up, they drove Jephthah out, and said to him, "You shall have no inheritance in our father's house, for you are the son of another woman."
                                        —JUDG. 11:1–2

Game's Closed!" used to be the slogan we yelled as kids when playing ball. We used it whenever a kid who was not particularly liked came upon a game. He was resigned to sit on the sidelines and watch the other kids play. It was a cruel move, socially. As temporary as it was, it was still rejection.

One of the most painful experiences in life to overcome is the trauma of rejection. Such was the case for Jephthah, who had no home to go to for love and affirmation. He was on his own, alone except for God. Where others rejected him, God adopted him and made him into a mighty man of valor. Jephthah had been hurt deeply and lived a hard life; he must have asked God why a thousand times. Yet he must have felt good when his rejecters finally came and begged for his help.

We cannot explain why we experience the pain and rejection that we do, but God knows and cares. Don't let the pain of rejection drive you away from others.

Lord, help us to see that the end of the matter is always better than the beginning when your hand is on us.

> *Do not be deceived: "Evil company corrupts*
> *good habits."*
> —1 COR. 15:33

Mitch was intense. It paid off in his business practice as he made a great deal of money honestly. It had shown up when he played professional football and went to a bowl several times.

He was so intense that if someone did not meet his need at the moment they went without attention from him. His wife felt it first. She felt abandoned in the raising of their four children. Mitch did not want to interact with her or the kids because the intensity of his day had consumed his relational skills. When he came home he only wanted to relax and reload for his responsibilities coming tomorrow.

So he and his wife stopped talking. After all, according to him, all she wanted to talk about was stuff she should handle. He did not come home and dump his business problems on her, did he?

They did not have problem children, but the family began to imitate Dad. The children became uptight and noncommunicative. His normally easygoing wife began to struggle with depression and anxiety. Mitch is still intense.

Do you know where your intensity goes? Or your impatience? Or your outbursts of anger?

Let love be without hypocrisy. Abhor what is evil.
Cling to what is good. —ROM. 12:9

Jim and Mary both had codependent backgrounds. They had denied their problems until their son, Jason, began to show some academic problems at school. They were then referred to me for counseling.

Both parents stressed that as good Christian parents they tried to give Jason the best. Both were successful in their chosen careers but made it a point to leave work on time to be with family. What they didn't tell me was that Jason was tired of his parents' going to church meetings. At first they couldn't see this as a problem, since they felt good about doing "God's work." Closer examination revealed that with his father being on two committees and his mother on several committees, Jason spent over 50 percent of his free time with a babysitter or in the church nursery.

Like many other well-meaning Christian parents, Jim and Mary failed to realize that workaholism doesn't stop once you leave the office. They had been deluded into thinking that because they left work on time everything was under control.

God, forgive me for using church as a cover-up for my drive to be perfect. Help me to gain control over my after-work activities so that I am more sensitive to the needs of my family.

> *"For this reason a man shall leave his father and mother and be joined to his wife."*
>
> —MARK 10:7

Mary felt guilty. She was suffering from the stress that comes from working and commuting in a large city. Home is usually a place of refuge, but not for Mary. Her daughter had just moved back home with a toddler. Mary had secretly looked forward to having free time after raising three kids. Now she was looking at family number two and she didn't have the energy to face the challenge.

The verse for today says that there is a "leaving" element to marriage and adulthood. The child is no longer a child and the parents are no longer responsible for them. The key word is *responsible*. If you find yourself in a similar situation, establish boundaries to keep responsibility where it belongs. Mary fell into the trap of taking too much responsibility for the rearing of her grandchild. As a result, her daughter did not develop responsibilities necessary for parenting, her husband felt neglected, and Mary burned out.

If you find yourself in this situation, set firm boundaries. Resist the temptation to take over for the kids. Take care of yourself. You have earned it.

Parents are not made of recyclable material.

So Jesus answered and said, "Were there not ten cleansed? But where are the nine?"

—LUKE 17:17

Julie was a complainer. Her family rarely did enough to earn her praise or gratitude. They always should have done things differently.

She came to counseling to find out what she could do to change them. That was not my assessment, that was her stated purpose. She saw their insensitivity and slowness as an infringement on her ability to become all she could be.

Julie knew she was not easy to live with. She knew she was impatient and ungrateful. But it was also true that the rest of the family was slow and insensitive and often did not listen well. She believed that if only they would change then she, too, would do better.

But the story of ten lepers whom Jesus cleansed does not validate that idea. All ten of these men were healed of their repulsive disease. All ten had their distasteful circumstances radically changed. But a change in circumstances did not make them grateful. If it had then all ten would have come back to say thank you. But only one did.

Circumstances change only circumstances. They do not change people.

Are you waiting for a change in circumstances to change your character?

> *There are many plans in a man's heart,*
> *Nevertheless the LORD's counsel—that will stand.*
> —PROV. 19:21

Today's Scripture text is a great reassurance as we try to maintain a more balanced life. Work addicts are always driven by an endless supply of plans. There are plans for every hour, day, and week of life. Each plan has a deadline, and a fear of not meeting the deadline generates more alternate plans. We are often obsessed with this process.

The verse from Proverbs reminds us that only God's purpose will occur in the final outcome. We should be good stewards of our time, talents, and money but not to the point where we are anxious and fearful.

I recommend keeping a prayer journal of plans that are committed to God and discussing your plans with others to get additional input. You can track your progress and see how much of what you do has a self-ish motive when you review your journal. I have found this prevents me from self-centered plans directed by my anxiety rather than God's purpose.

Lord, thank you for having a master plan for my life. Help me always to take comfort in that and use my mind to seek your plan.

And Jesus answered and said to her, "Martha, Martha, you are worried and troubled about many things."
                                              —LUKE 10:41

Sweet little Lily. She was such a kindly, pleasant lady. She simply beamed when her house was spotless. She seemed to desire nothing more from life than to prepare banquets for her family, to do their laundry and other chores, and to work a full-time job besides. Little did anyone know that beneath that kind and gentle exterior dwelled a raging workaholic. One day when Lily related her hectic schedule to me I asked, "When do you relax?" "Relax?" she exclaimed incredulously. "Who has time to relax?" There it was—the workaholic was drawn out of the closet.

We must be careful not to stereotype the workaholic as a male who goes off to work, does twelve hours, comes home, and collapses into bed. Moms are some of the most blatant workaholics to be found. Most are surrounded by irresponsible children and husbands who are taking advantage of the situation. Many mothers are *always* tired but never delegate, rationalizing that it is "easier to do it myself."

Anything done in excess is displeasing to God and harmful to ourselves.

Lord, help us learn from Jesus' message to Martha.

> *Blessed be the God and Father of our Lord Jesus*
> *Christ, who has blessed us with every spiritual*
> *blessing in the heavenly places in Christ.*
> —EPH. 1:3

She did not know about blessing. Louise looked at her life and was convinced that she had been cursed. At a young age and for many years she had experienced incest. The man in her life who should have protected her was the one who hurt her most severely.

The sad result was that Louise grappled with two contradictory messages. The obvious one said she was worthless, "damaged goods." The other came from deep within and said that regardless of what others had done to her, she was not a horrible person. The deep-down message usually lost.

Louise struggled with a seriously wounded picture of herself. To be sure, she was a believer in Christ. She was thankful that he offered salvation. But that seemed to be reserved for the "sweet by and by" and did not change the present.

We began to work on her thinking process the first day we met. For example, she took today's verse and said, "Thank you, God, that you have blessed me with every blessing that is in heaven. I do not feel like you have, and I cannot see it, but thank you that it is true."

The truest thing about Louise was what the Scripture said, not what she felt or had experienced. How well do you know that?

*And do not be conformed to this world, but be
transformed by the renewing of your mind.*
—ROM. 12:2

Garbage in, garbage out." We hear it all the time from
computer people. It is the recognition of the fact that
computers make very accurate mistakes if they have
been programmed with mistakes—garbage, if you will.
Louise had been programmed with garbage. At an im-
pressionable age she had repeatedly heard that she
was just a body to be used and her feelings did not
matter.

We had been working on her thinking process for
about a month before I called it "reprogramming." It is
the only road to transformation, and Louise knew she
needed to be transformed from what the incest had
done to her.

The process of renewing the mind has two steps.
The first is to recognize the lies and the inaccurate self-
talk. The second step is to replace the lies with the
truth. The problem is that the lies are subtle and the
replacement takes more than a single corrective act.

---

*Focus on step one for today. Ask God to show you any lies or "gar-
bage" that your computer, your mind, treats as truth. The thoughts
may regard what you think about yourself, other people, circumstances, or even God himself.*

For we walk by faith, not by sight.
—2 COR. 5:7

For Louise to renew her mind she had to replace many thoughts that had "seniority," and they were not going to be easily changed.

One such belief was the constant message that she was not good enough, no matter what she did. As a result she was always trying harder and harder and, quite honestly, was doing quite well. But her belief system would not allow her to see her doing well at anything.

To change that idea she had to take certain ideas as truth, not because she could see that they were true but because she would choose to believe they were true. She had to replace her standards of measurement.

She had two options. One was what trustworthy family and friends could say to her was true. The other was what Scripture said about her.

Louise was eventually able to trust a small number of people who could be counted on to speak honestly to her. She also began to choose to believe Scripture verses that spoke of her worth and value. She did not discount those just because her emotions did not verify them.

Louise improved because she replaced some negative thoughts and beliefs. Do you have any parts that need replacement?

Finally, brethren, whatever things are true,
whatever things are noble, whatever things are
just, whatever things are pure, whatever things
are lovely . . . meditate on these things.

—PHIL. 4:8

Recovery was frustrating for Lee. One of his largest battles was his negative thinking. When he started to work less and spend more time with his family, he was convinced that financial disaster was imminent and that he would lose everything, including his family. His family reassured him but it did not help. Instead he would rationalize that they were only saying that to make him feel better.

Negative thinking is a common characteristic of workaholics and members of their families. It is promoted by perfectionism and an unconscious belief that it is possible to know and be in control of everything. When this doesn't happen disappointment fuels negative thoughts.

Lee was unable to look at his life choices realistically and with promise. He was drained of the energy he needed to do his work and manage his life by this negative thinking.

Negative thoughts are unnecessary and unproductive.

> *Search me, O God, and know my heart;*
> *Try me, and know my anxieties;*
> *And see if there is any wicked way in me,*
> *And lead me in the way everlasting.*
>
> —PS. 139:23

What is the most acute pain you have ever experienced? Some have said the passing of kidney stones, third-degree burns, torn ligaments, cancer. I certainly do not want to find out firsthand, do you? The focus of today's thought is on an area of moral pain, which can be much worse than physical pain. I recently saw *The Godfather III*. If you haven't followed the story it is about a Mafia family led by Michael Corleone. His life of crime and murder catches up with him, emotionally and morally, to the point that he would do anything to be rid of his past and the resultant pain.

This prayer of David is a classic verse of Scripture. David still experienced the moral pain of his actions through his family. But the real reason for his recovery from a more painful life was the grace of God in his life and David's willingness to cooperate with him. It is guaranteed: pray this verse daily and you will be spared the most excruciating pain of all—moral pain.

Lord, help us to cooperate with you as David did.

Hide Your face from my sins,
And blot out all my iniquities.
Create in me a clean heart, O God,
And renew a steadfast spirit within me.
                                        —PS. 51:9–10

An important concept of the Twelve Step program is our powerlessness to change and God's ability to change us. After we admit our wrongs we come to Step Six of the program: "Were entirely ready to have God remove all these defects of character."

The key points in this step are: 1) We must be *ready* to be changed. That means being mentally prepared to face what we need to face. 2) We must acknowledge that it is God who transforms our character. It is important to note that he can never do it without our cooperation. So cooperate with him!

The verse for today comes from that great psalm of repentance written by David after his heinous sin with Bathsheba. David and millions of others have found the release from bondage they desired when they turned control over to God.

Lord, help us to understand that he who loses his life for your sake shall find it.

> *But exhort one another daily, while it is called "Today."*
> —HEB. 3:13

I enjoy tinkering under the hood of my car to keep it running. Extensive repairs are out of my league, but minor tune-ups and oil changes are within the realm of my limited expertise.

Fram Filters had a great commercial that said, "Pay me now or pay me later." The scene showed a garage mechanic comparing the cost of purchasing an oil filter from him today to the cost of having him overhaul an entire engine that had worn out because of dirty oil. The filter is obviously much cheaper than the engine overhaul.

Most obsessives think they can violate that principle. They tend to think they can get away with neglecting maintenance on relationships and not have to pay for it later in severely damaged family and friends.

But the Fram man is right. To keep personal relationships healthy, I can only choose when to pay, not whether or not to pay. If I neglect my primary relationships because I do not have the time today, it may cost me dearly later.

When was the last time you did some relationship maintenance? Do any of your relationships need overhauling?

*For in the multitude of dreams and many words
there is also vanity. But fear God.*

—ECCL. 5:7

Tony's wife came in for counseling after separating from him. She was bitter and had been hurt many times by his absence from home and his periods of unfaithfulness throughout their marriage. She felt Tony's attitudes about work were key to understanding him. She characterized Tony as a dreamer. Although she felt he was very gifted in terms of his talents underneath he was insecure about this. She said Tony was always complaining about the professional people for whom he did construction work. He would complain that they got all the breaks and didn't have to do "real work" like he did. His wife would suggest he change fields but he would deny his competency.

Instead he was motivated by a dream—if he worked long enough and hard enough he would eventually make enough money to buy all the things for his family that his customers had.

Tony's wife loved him very much but she was tired of colluding in The Dream. Unless he could give up his obsessive future thinking and face his life in the present, his addiction would destroy him.

Do you compare yourself to others and devalue yourself? Do you frequently talk about the future to numb your present pain?

For wisdom is a defense as money is a defense,
But . . . wisdom gives life to those who have it.
—ECCL. 7:12

When I met with Tony he was devastated that his wife had left him. He felt both angry and guilty—angry because he was working as hard as he could and felt she should be able to understand, but guilty because he knew that he had made promises he never kept.

He told me about The Dream. His father had ingrained the work ethic into him from an early age: "If you want to get ahead you have to work hard." Tony respected his father but was unaware of the impact his father's absence had had on his attitudes about life and work.

Tony revealed that he felt insecure about his intellect and chose not to explore other career fields. Instead, he threw himself physically into his work. In the evenings he would try to stay ahead of his competitors by staying out past work hours to get bids. All of this was to fulfill The Dream, to someday make his family happy.

Father, help me to accept my responsibility for what I need to do today and to reconcile with my past.

My soul melts from heaviness;
Strengthen me according to Your Word.
Remove from me the way of lying,
And grant me Your law graciously.
—PS. 119:28–29

Tony was learning that he avoided painful feelings by overemphasizing the physical. Because he felt he was inadequate intellectually he would work very hard physically to prove he was a *man*.

As he got older and couldn't keep up with the younger men, he felt the bad feelings and had to keep them numb. He found himself avoiding home and frequenting the local tavern where there were sympathetic ears and plenty of alcohol to keep the bad feelings at bay.

As his body deteriorated and his anxiety increased sex became his other cross-addiction. Since he felt inadequate in the presence of his wife he turned to other women for validation. This, of course, was the last straw for his wife. Tony now realized that The Dream had crumbled. He knew he had to face his pain if there was any hope of his wife's returning.

How do cross-addictions to alcohol, sex, or other people keep you from facing your problems?

Now may our Lord Jesus Christ Himself . . .
comfort your hearts and establish you in every
good word and work. —2 THESS. 2:16–17

Tony's recovery was not easy. First, he had to break out of his denial and face the negative feelings of anger, fear, and hurt he had worked all his life to bury. He also had to develop a more balanced view of his father so that he could begin to face some of his own unmet needs. Finally, he had to learn how to level with his wife and seek her forgiveness for the pain he had caused her.

Giving up The Dream was one of the places where Tony fought recovery the most. To give this up meant that he had to learn to take responsibility for his life in the present. As Tony progressed he learned that God had forgiven him long ago, even when he couldn't forgive himself. He was able to let go of the burden The Dream put on him, and began to redefine career goals that worked for him and his family.

———————

Lord, help me to give up harmful and unproductive practices so that I can move forward in my life.

For though I am free from all men, I have made
myself a servant to all, that I might win the more.
. . . I have become all things to all men, that I
might by all means save some.
—1 COR. 9:19, 22

Recently my wife and I visited the Middle East, and we thoroughly enjoyed the intriguing culture. Veiled women and men wearing turbans were the absolute norm. Westerners were the only exception.

Something happened on the plane that we found most enlightening. We boarded along with Arab men and women dressed in veils and robes. However, shortly after takeoff a veiled Arab woman would enter a bathroom and then emerge wearing a stylish Western dress. Likewise an Arab man dressed in robe and turban would enter the lavatory and be transformed into an international businessman wearing a three-piece suit. The reverse of this procedure had taken place on our flight into the Middle East.

These Arabs had learned that to operate outside their own culture they had to set aside certain garb for a short time.

A workaholic cannot set aside his own beliefs for any length of time. He sees only two options to any situation: his way and the wrong way.

Do you need to "change clothes" every now and then? Do you need to consider someone else's point of view more often than you now do?

*And His disciples asked Him, saying, "Rabbi, who
sinned, this man or his parents, that he was born
blind?"*
                                        —JOHN 9:2

I never knew how much of a rageaholic my father was
until we removed the pictures from the walls during
the move to our new house," Debbie said. "How's
that?" I inquired. "Mom hung the pictures over holes
punched in the wall by Dad when he had a fit," she
said. Her mom did a good job of covering up for her
dad.

What a picture Debbie described! Can you see her
dad punching the wall in a fit of frustration and rage,
then slinking away in guilt and shame after he realized
what he had done? Can you see her mom dutifully, si-
lently, appearing with a picture and nailing it over the
hole? Can you see her mom then going about her business as if nothing had taken place?

Debbie described a family that keeps secrets. How
was she hurt by this particular secret? As a child she
thought that Mom hid the holes from her because she
caused Dad to get angry and go into a rage. Debbie
thought, "I will try to be a better girl for you, Dad, I
promise." She has spent her adult life trying to be that
better girl by achieving and overworking. Is it not
great to know that God does not condemn us as we
tend to condemn ourselves?

———————

Children are good observers—but poor interpreters!

Do not remember the former things,
Nor consider the things of old.
Behold, I will do a new thing,
Now it shall spring forth;
Shall you not know it?
—ISA. 43:18–19

During the Persian Gulf War the Allied Forces were constantly informed of Iraq's use of the SCUD missiles. At first these missiles were feared to be very dangerous, but later we learned that our Patriot missiles were in most instances able to intercept and destroy them.

In many ways we have our own symbolic internal missile war going on. Negative self-talk, which is the language we use to support a negative self-image, can be thought of as our SCUDs. These missiles serve only to inflict damage to our psyche by causing us to believe that we are not good enough.

To recover from work addictions we need to develop our own internal Patriot missile defense. We can respond to our negative emotions of anger, fear, and hurt with new, positive messages, such as "I am lovable in Christ," or "God wants to meet my needs."

Lord, do not allow negative self-talk to rule me, but instead free me from its power.

> *"Father, if it is Your will, remove this cup from Me;*
> *nevertheless not My will, but Yours, be done."*
> —LUKE 22:42

Linda had found the man of her dreams. He was everything she had ever imagined. They had so much in common: both had the same spiritual beliefs, both had similar goals for life, and neither wanted to be mediocre in anything he or she did.

A proposal had been made, and it appeared that a date would soon be set and a permanent relationship formally established.

The only problem was that he did not think she was the one for him. There had been a proposal, all right. She had proposed to him. And when his response did not match hers, she began to try all the harder to prove to him what a good match they made. The more she pushed, the further he moved from her.

Linda suffered from a common obsessive condition: tunnel vision. Very likely you are saying to yourself that you would never do something as extreme as this. In the area of choosing a marriage partner that is probably true. But are other areas of your life just enough out of your control that you can see them from only one perspective—yours?

Pray the prayer of Jesus Christ himself, "Not my will but yours be done."

The LORD opens the eyes of the blind;
The LORD raises those who are bowed down;
The LORD loves the righteous. —PS. 146:8

Anne Wilson Schaef refers to one of the characteristics of addictive individuals and their families as *tunnel vision*, the inability to focus attention in more than one direction at a time.

A workaholic may be home with his family and direct his attention to any family member in what appears to be appropriate interaction. The problem occurs later when this individual has to change focus. He then treats those with whom he may have just interacted as if they don't exist; in fact, this is how he thinks.

Tunnel vision also operates in reference to new ideas or changes in routine. An addict lacks the ability to be flexible and adjust his own thinking.

Certainly there are those times when it is appropriate to be firm when confronted with change. However, when we become rigid or dogmatic something is out of balance.

Observe how you interact with those around you this week; notice how you react to change.

Through the LORD's mercies we are not consumed,
Because His compassions fail not.
They are new every morning;
Great is Your faithfulness.
—LAM. 3:22

A businessman once placed his five-year-old son on the table and told the boy to jump to him. The boy, hesitant at first, finally took the leap of faith after his father's coaxing. As the boy sailed through the air the father stepped aside, allowing him to plummet to the ground. The son looked up at his dad with a hurt and confused look. His father said, "Son, let that be a lesson to you—never trust anyone!"

Unfortunately, we all receive that message in one form or another. Some of us have been so hurt that we have put up a wall so that no one can reach us. However, God did not intend for us to live in isolation. We choose such a lifestyle because we are afraid to trust.

How do you overcome mistrust? You usually need help from someone who will help you set boundaries, and will look out for your best interests. Professional counseling can certainly help. And, the Lord, too, will help you if you trust in him.

If God seems distant, check to see who moved!

Wait on the LORD;
Be of good courage,
And He shall strengthen your heart;
Wait, I say, on the LORD!
—PS. 27:14

James and David hated to wait. We were living in southern Africa at the time, and they were new to our location. They had not yet bought a car, so I had driven them to their assignment about a week before. I was surprised when they hitchhiked the twenty-two miles to my office.

Their request was much more surprising: they wanted to go home. They were discouraged by the work to be done and they doubted their ability.

I tried to remind them that they were pioneers, that it had been tough for me at first, too. I suggested they give it another week, and if no change took place by then they could go to the airport. They agreed and I drove them back to their home.

That was about fifteen years ago and they are both still in Africa. They absolutely love it and are both extremely effective. They chose to wait on the Lord.

Today pray, "Lord, show me where I need to wait for you."

Do not overwork to be rich;
Because of your own understanding, cease!
—PROV. 23:4

Sal said he worked hard in order to be successful. On the surface this sounded normal, but to Sal, success was everything. Every choice he made was focused on this goal. Even Sal's first marriage took place so that he could promote himself as a successful family man.

Sal started his career by owning and operating his own service station. He spent all his time making that a success but eventually sold the business because he had moved up as far as he could. Without the fix offered by the "success carrot" Sal had to create his own new challenge. His wife had always lived with the hope that he gave her that once the business stabilized they would get more time together. She divorced him when he then started his own contracting business. Sal again put all his energy into being successful. During this time he married again. And once again, when he had expanded this business as far as he could he moved on but this time left $300,000 of debt. Sal was blinded by success and was in denial because he was "living the high life."

It is often difficult for us to distinguish between ambition and addiction. Pray for the wisdom to know the difference.

The Lord takes pleasure in those who fear Him,
In those who hope in His mercy.

—PS. 147:11

By the time Sal came in for therapy his second wife was ready to leave him. He was very frustrated by this and thought she was being unreasonable. After all, he was more successful than ever. He couldn't understand why she kept harping on their relationship. She complained that he needed her only for a "showpiece" when his company had a party.

When I explored Sal's background I learned that he was an adult child of an alcoholic (ACOA). He quickly became uncomfortable when I asked him about his parents. He tended to paint them in idealistic fashion as "loving and close." I had learned from his wife in private that Sal was the oldest in his family and frequently had to help take care of the younger siblings because of his father's dysfunction. He apparently had vowed as a child that he would be a success so that his family would not have to suffer.

Sal never returned for therapy and as far as I know is still in denial. He is now three million dollars in debt, but has no problems because he was a success!

Pray for peaceful resolution of your past.

*Then I hated all my labor in which I had toiled
under the sun, because I must leave it to the
man who will come after me.*   —ECCL. 2:18

A client of mine could not understand why she felt so
burned out since she recently cut her workload back to
"ten or eleven hours a day, which is nothing." When I
told her she might be a workaholic she immediately
denied it because she did not enjoy her work.

People work for different reasons. Some do it to create to the best of their God-given abilities; this motivation is probably the closest to God's design. Others
work because it is their life. They have no other desires
or interests; they are single-minded. Others work because they are driven by the ghosts of the past. They
are attempting to live up to some impossible standard
and feel they have no choice about it.

Solomon, the author of today's verse, set out to accomplish incredible feats to answer the question of the
meaning of life. He acquired great wealth and accomplished incredible tasks. He concluded that after it was
all said and done he would leave his wealth behind to
someone else.

Lord, help us to work for the right reasons.

*Not that I speak in regard to need, for I have
learned in whatever state I am, to be content.*
—PHIL. 4:11

Dennis was an achiever. He had been top salesman in
the nation in his entire industry, not just his company,
for two years in a row. He knew his product and how to
sell it honestly.

But Dennis was a perfectionist. He did spend time
with his family, but they wished he was on the road
more. When he came home the kids were too loud, too
slow, too talkative, too impatient, not quick enough to
obey him, or they would not talk to him enough.

His wife was a total failure. The house was not clean
enough. She usually overspent on her budget which he
had set for her. She could not satisfy him in bed. She
was too fat; she needed to lose 10 more pounds and get
under 105 pounds. She did not initiate enough, and she
was not romantic or sexy enough. Because she did not
seem thrilled at the end of a sexual encounter he
sensed she was telling him he was an inadequate lover.

Dennis could not see that he was the common denominator in all these problem relationships.

*How content are you with your relationships? What is the common
denominator in the problem areas of your life?*

*For not he who commends himself is approved, but
whom the Lord commends.* —2 COR. 10:18

Dennis was vulnerable to a disease common to perfectionists. He was stricken by comparisonism. He
compared what his boss did to what he thought his
boss should do. He was comparing his boss to himself
and, of course, his boss lost in the comparison.

He did the same with his children's behavior. It was
what Dennis saw vs. what Dennis thought he should
see.

When he did it to his wife he guaranteed that she
could not satisfy him sexually. He knew that he was a
good lover, because he had experience before they
were married. She was the problem, because he had
been with better lovers than she was. She was frigid.
He reminded her of that frequently.

All his comparisons were unrealistic. In each case he
compared a real person to an imagination or fantasy. It
was never reality vs. reality.

*How much do you compare reality with fantasy? Who seems to
always win when you compare?*

His divine power has given to us all things
that pertain to life and godliness, through
the knowledge of Him who called us by
glory and virtue.   —2 PETER 1:3

Dennis's wife, Patty, came to see me initially. She did not know what else she or the children could do to please him. With the children she tried to balance the negative messages from Dennis with positive messages from her. It helped a little, but it only covered the symptom and not the root.

Dealing with herself was a different issue. Patty was beginning to believe that something was wrong with her sexually and that she was beyond hope. In reality, the problem was not what Dennis was saying but that she was beginning to believe it.

Rebuilding her self-esteem was slow but consistent. We started with the irrefutable truth that God had given her everything she needed for life and godliness. Because neither her feelings nor her husband's opinion validated that fact, she had to choose to believe it before growth began to show.

What was true for Patty is also true for you. No matter what anyone says about you, if there is a relationship with God, then you have already been given everything you need for life and godliness.

Therefore, my beloved, as you have always obeyed,
not as in my presence only, but now much more in
my absence, work out your own salvation with fear
and trembling.   —PHIL. 2:12

Before Patty's true value could be seen in her behavior, it first had to be recognized by her. She had to grasp the fact that this comes about as a result of obedience, as the verse says.

Patty and I searched for what was true about her. We reviewed what trusted friends had said about her. She wrote down what her children thought about her mothering. Though it was painful, I had her recall why Dennis had said he wanted to marry her.

For Patty the "obedience" had much more to do with what she *believed* than what she *did*. One of her assignments was to personalize Psalm 139. In this process she would read what David wrote about God's view of him, as though it were God's view of her. In reality, God's view of David is the same as his view of Patty and everyone who has a personal relationship with him.

Do you indeed have such a personal relationship with God? Do you believe what he says about you or what some mere human says about you?

*And do not be drunk with wine, in which is
dissipation; but be filled with the Spirit.*
—EPH. 5:18

Dennis had been an addict for some time. His list of
addictions was longer than most, not as long as some.
He was addicted to money, control, rage, power, sex,
self-gratification, work, prestige, exercise, appear-
ances, and materialism, to name most of his excesses.

It took a lot of work to develop all those addictions.
He was not born addicted to all those things, and the
process through which he went is worthy of our attention.

To begin with, something happened in Dennis's
life that caused him pain. Usually it is either one mas-
sive traumatic event or the cumulative effect of many
small though painful experiences. For Dennis it was
the latter. He grew up in a family where roles were
mixed or unclear, and demands placed on him were
unrealistic. He felt the pain of being raised in a dysfunctional family.

How are you looking for relief from your pain right now?

*Please refer to the Addictive Cycle chart on p. 367 while reading this series
of devotionals.

> *If a man is blameless . . . not accused of dissipation*
> *or insubordination.*
> —TITUS 1:6

Dennis looked to substances for relief. In college he used alcohol and other drugs. Drugs work to numb pain, to anesthetize. Whether the pain is physical, emotional, or even spiritual, enough of any drug will provide relief. And it worked for Dennis.

But eventually it always wore off, so he went to other substances on the list. Next he tried sex to counter his pain. By its very nature, sex normally gives pleasure which counteracts pain. But the law of diminishing returns soon goes into effect. Then, the person requires more sex, or more partners, to the point of extreme distortion in order to achieve the same pain relief. It is not sex for sex. It becomes sex for release from pain.

In college people said Dennis was wild. But in fact he was only using what was available to anesthetize his pain. When I suggested that this explained his behavior back then, he rejected the idea. He was a man. He had never run from pain.

I often ask myself what I ask you now: are you running from some pain in a way that does not look like running?

In regard to these, they think it strange that you do not run with them in the same flood of dissipation, speaking evil of you.   **—1 PETER 4:4**

Soon after graduation from college Dennis developed an interest in spiritual things and professed a belief in Jesus Christ. As is often the case, continual use of any substance to numb pain brings on its own source of pain. That had been true for Dennis, so he began to break away from some of the excesses that were more obviously harmful.

But he was still an addict; his substances of choice just changed. He began to exercise his addictive tendencies on the compulsions America applauds. He began to make money, earn power, and control people. These efforts, too, helped to numb the pain.

Work was central for him. He had always worked very hard. As a child he had had to in order to avoid severe punishment from his parents. But as a child his hard work never earned him anything. Such was not the case in the business world. There his perfectionism earned him attention, envy from others, raises, and promotions. So he became addicted to work because of what he earned from working. The money was only a nice fringe benefit.

How do you view your work? Is it a means to pay the bills or does it do something more for you?

Let your conduct be without covetousness, and be content with such things as you have. For He Himself has said, "I will never leave you nor forsake you."
—HEB. 13:5

Due to his perfectionism, Dennis began to rise above his peers in the business world and received the financial and material benefits accorded him. Once that happened, his love for money began to vie for control in his life.

He always had to have a new car every year. But even that was not enough, and he then needed the very first model of a car each year.

Then he needed a house at the beach, but not just any house would do. It had to be the best. But because it was the best, the kids could not really enjoy it. They might mess something up, or ruin the carpet, or clog the drain. So now the family dreaded vacations to the beach.

In reality, he did not own either his car or his beach house: they owned him. The saddest part of Dennis's story was that he was a believer in God who said, "I will never leave you nor forsake you."

Do you have anything that owns you? Is some possession so valuable that you cannot do without it?

*Flee also from youthful lusts; but pursue
righteousness, faith, love, peace with those
who call on the Lord out of a pure heart.*
—2 TIM. 2:22

Dennis followed the pattern of most addicts, moving from one substance to another. Sometimes he left behind the old, ineffective substance, but usually he carried some vestige of the old on to the next substance. That was the case with his sexual addiction.

He never really left his compulsion toward sex. Though for the first several years of marriage he was "technically faithful" to Patty, he continually fantasized being with other, more exciting women. When that did not give him the "buzz" he sought, he turned to pornographic magazines.

All of this occurred while he professed belief in Christ, taught Bible studies, and was a leader in their church. The problem reached its peak when he began using call girls on his out of town trips. Three months later he planned a trip to the city where an old girlfriend lived and renewed their sexual relationship.

Are there any signs of this subtle slide taking place in your sexual life? The good news is that pure motivation from the heart is all the Lord says is necessary for him to help. Step one is to flee.

> *Let no corrupt communication proceed out of your*
> *mouth, but what is good for necessary edification,*
> *that it may impart grace to the hearers.*
> —EPH. 4:29

Of all his addictions, the most damaging to himself and to others was rage. With his tongue he wounded his wife, children, and subordinates. Indirectly he would make cuts at his boss and clients.

His rage was always rationalized. It was always someone else who "made" him mad. At first he could not grasp the fact that no one could "make" him mad, they could only reveal the anger that was already inside him.

Because of his quick mind, he could make Patty look like an idiot. With his children, he used his anger and rage to discipline, control, and punish. His children tended to remember only *how* he said things, not *what* he said. Patty only remembered the strong feelings of being used and manipulated. Because of her insecurities, she personalized his abusive speech and anger and became bitter toward him.

Rage expressed always creates a deadly cycle. Have you determined who is responsible for your anger?

> *"Today, if you will hear His voice,*
> *Do not harden your hearts as in the rebellion."*
> —HEB. 3:15

Years of blaming others had hardened Dennis's heart. Though we worked for several months, he denied that he could be responsible for the problems at home, work, and church. He was convinced that the explanation for his sexual frustration was his wife's frigidity.

He truly believed he was not at fault. He never took Step One: he never acknowledged that he was in need. He never could admit to being weak or inadequate in any area, though that fact was painfully obvious to everyone who knew him.

Dennis started to travel to cities where old girlfriends lived. He eventually left his wife and children. He is no longer top salesman for his company, much less the industry itself. His church requested that he deal with his problems before returning to fellowship with them again. Though the process was gradual, his heart became so hard that it is now brittle. He also has few friends, and no intimate relationships. The old girlfriends quickly tired of being used.

Dear God, please keep my heart pliable. Do not let me become deceived due to my own hardness of heart.

[They] exchanged the truth of God for the lie, and worshiped and served the creature rather than the Creator, who is blessed forever. Amen.
—ROM 1:25

At the root of each of Dennis's addictions was idolatry. He was willing to pay any price to gratify his desires. We have called them addictions for many years, but they are actually "idols."

Whether it was drugs, money, sex, work, or rage, Dennis was substituting a substance to do one of two things. He was either trying to meet a legitimate need in an illegitimate way, as was the case with sex. Or he was trying to gratify a desire which was not a legitimate right, as was the situation with how he used his rage to gain control. The control was not his to own.

Idolatry is a spiritual problem. The pain was merely a symptom, and the addictions were a temporary means of dealing with a symptom.

Often the addiction needs attention. It needs to be extinguished. But to give attention only to temporary solutions and avoid the spiritual aspects is to put a bandage on a wound needing surgery.

In your pain, what are you solving? Are you dealing with symptoms or roots?

"For behold, I create Jerusalem as a rejoicing,
And her people a joy." —ISA. 65:18

Sid's wife, Margaret, was embarrassed and angry as a result of her husband's behavior at the corporate golf tournament.

Sid was the president of his company. On the day of the golf game the group he and Margaret were in had agreed to play nine holes for what was to be a friendly game. Instead, because of Sid, they ended up playing a very competitive eighteen-hole match in one-hundred-degree weather.

When they teed off Margaret's ball was the shortest shot. The other golfers in the group all suggested they set a stroke limit to keep the group moving. Sid adamantly opposed this and insisted they play by the rules. Since Sid was the boss no one said anything.

When the group finally approached the ninth hole Sid wanted to play another nine holes. Everyone protested about the heat and commented on how tired his wife looked. Once again, however, the boss ruled. Margaret was so humiliated she didn't care if she never played golf again.

Like most workaholics, Sid worked at his play and made it very competitive. Look at the way you play and ask yourself if others enjoy playing with you.

And He said to them, "Take heed and beware of covetousness, for one's life does not consist in the abundance of the things he possesses."
—LUKE 12:15

The late Vince Lombardi, coach of the Green Bay Packers, was known for his ability to motivate men. He enabled his players to perform beyond their perceived capabilities. He carried such respect that he could push and berate a "goldbricking" linebacker twice his size without considering the consequences of making him angry. His best-known saying is often misapplied, unfortunately: "Winning isn't everything, It's the only thing."

What inferences can you draw from such a statement? If you do not always win you lose? Your life is measured by the successes and losses you experience? It does not matter how you play the game as long as you come out on top? All of these inferences are wrong, because winning at any cost is never the road to fulfillment. Many a person has learned that unfortunate truth too late.

Winning is fun; it sure beats losing every time. I highly recommend it—but not at the cost of personal integrity. Our lives consist of more than what we possess, trophies included.

―――――――――

It is more important to win the war than to win the battle.

Lead me in Your truth and teach me,
For You are the God of my salvation.
—PS. 25:5

Leo was devastated and in a state of shock as he sat staring at the pink slip from his division vice president. "I can't be fired! This has never happened to me before. I have given some of the best years of my career to this organization." Leo's mind raced on the day he hit bottom.

Leo was a competent project manager with a large engineering company. However, over the past two years his superiors and co-workers had complained that he was pushing his subordinates too hard. Leo denied this was a problem and would use the "bottom line" as his rationale.

The truth was that people were clamoring to get transferred to another project. The only reason the deadlines were met was because Leo put in long hours to cover for what he termed his "incompetent co-workers." His superiors didn't argue with the results at first, but now the workload was more than he could possibly do alone.

The first step of recovery is admitting our helplessness to control excess work.

> *Every good gift and every perfect gift is from above.*
> —JAMES 1:17

Most people have heard the McDonald's slogan, "You deserve a break today!" The implication is that today you have worked hard and now it is time to reward yourself. Sounds good, doesn't it? It's sold a lot of hamburgers too.

But implicit in the slogan is that what has been done *is* deserving of this break. That is fine if the standard being used is realistic. If the measurement compares reality and fantasy, reality will lose every time.

Applying this to a workaholic, McDonald's is *not* who will determine whether a break is deserved today. That privilege is reserved for the workaholic himself, and he usually has such unattainable standards that breaks are undeserved, even if taken.

The reason the death of Jesus is often called the "good news" is because the Scripture promises a "break"—salvation—as a result of a gift, not because we deserve it.

Gifts can be tough to receive. A gift has its foundation in the giver, not the recipient.

———————————

How about you? Have you received this gift or are you still working at deserving it?

Hope in God, for I shall yet praise Him
For the help of His countenance.

—PS. 42:5

It had been nearly six months since the near-fatal collision for Keith. All he remembers before impact was saying to himself, "Just one more sales call and I will exceed my quota for the ninth straight month."

The accident dramatically altered Keith's life. He had been off work for a total of four months and was by his standards only at 60 percent of normal. Keith never realized his addictive qualities until he was removed from work, his primary addiction. As he faced both his physical and emotional pain he realized he had made a shambles of his life. His disability insurance covered only some of his expenses, and Keith realized he had become dependent on his working to cover his overextended line of credit.

He was extremely depressed when he started the men's group but slowly began to receive hope and encouragement from others. Tim was particularly helpful when he explained that it was bankruptcy that brought him down, but that he owed his recovery to his newfound faith in Christ. This helped Keith face his fear of bankruptcy.

Christ is the true higher power to deliver us from our false gods of work, power, and success.

> *Pray for us; for we are confident that we have a*
> *good conscience, in all things desiring to live*
> *honorably.*
> —HEB. 13:18

I called the office of a businessman one day. His secretary said that he was not in the office at the moment, and asked if I'd care to leave a message. I said yes and told her who I was. She said, "Oh, one minute please, he was expecting your call." A moment later the man was on the phone. I didn't raise the issue but I knew what was going on. The secretary was not lying, but she was not telling the truth either.

There are black lies and there are white lies. Black lies are lies that are conscious and purposely deceiving. White lies are half-truths that were known in biblical times as guile. They contain just enough truth to ease the conscience.

We must realize that honesty is not a part-time thing and guile is not a harmless act. We must be committed to honesty, and the determination must come from within. Maintaining integrity is never the easiest way, but it is the most rewarding.

Are you a merchant of guile? Can you unhesitantly say with our verse for today that you desire to live honorably, whatever the cost?

One of the simple pleasures of life is to lay your head on the pillow at night with a clear conscience.

*"For whoever desires to save his life will lose it, and
whoever loses his life for My sake will find it."*
—MATT. 16:25

Brad was thirty, good looking, and made $120,000 a
year selling electronic appliances! Brad had broken
every sales record on the East Coast and could date
any woman he wanted. All those around him suggested he was in yuppie heaven, but he said he was
bored. "How can I be depressed when I have it all?" he
asked.

Brad's history revealed addictions to work, exercise,
and women. He sought out our clinic because he
wanted "ethical" counseling and seemed offended that
I would suggest he had addiction problems. I based my
observations on several facts. The first was that his career goals were all external motivations. He wanted to
be the best in sales nationally no matter how many
hours he had to work. The second fact was that Brad
was in excellent physical shape but constantly set
higher performance goals for himself as a biker. Finally, he described relationships with only helpless
women. He would rescue them and then get bored.

---

*Brad had wanted a quick fix to numb his boredom. How does work
numb your emotions?*

> *For all have sinned and fall short of the glory of*
> *God, being justified freely by His grace through the*
> *redemption that is in Christ Jesus.*
> —ROM. 3:23–24

Brad had joined a support group at my recommendation and was trying to work his Twelve Step program.
He now admitted he was hopelessly out of control and
needed God's help.

Brad had always considered himself religious. Many
of the others in his group, however, talked as if God
were very personal and spoke as if they actually could
give God control over their compulsions. I then asked
Brad if he was interested in trading in yuppie heaven
for the real thing. He was attentive to this and I proceeded to ask him what he would tell God if God asked
him why he should let him into heaven. He nervously
tried to justify some reasons based on his previous
"moral" living, but he eventually conceded that it probably wasn't enough.

Brad and I were then able to explore the third step
of his recovery—deciding to let God have control over
all areas of his life. In Brad's case this meant giving up
the false gods of wealth, success, and the perfect-
looking body and trusting God to guide him through
recovery.

———————

Step Three of recovery is probably the most important because, as
we remove our addictions from our life, we give God control over the
outcome.

*For even when we were with you, we commanded
you this: If any will not work, neither shall he eat.*
—2 THESS. 3:10

Workaholaphobia is the fear of becoming a workaholic. Actually, there is no such term—I made it up. I
have observed the phenomenon, however. It is caused
by working with recovering workaholics. George is a
former pastor who has gone into teaching. He had invested so much in his church that he physically and
emotionally burned out. Now in recovery he has
learned how to say no and how to delegate. He
preached balance to his staff and warned them of the
danger of overwork. Unfortunately, his staff overre-
acted to what he said. They became concerned that
they were burning out whenever they had to work
hard and long on a project. They became fearful of
workaholism.

It's hard to find the balance between a good day's
work and the drive to overwork. The best way to tell if
it is a healthy work ethic is to examine your motive for
work. If your motivation is greed, insecurity, or validation of self-worth, it is a compulsion. If it is to work for
the sake of accomplishment, it is probably healthy.

Lord, help us not to fear what is good for us.

> *Casting all your care upon Him, for He cares*
> *for you.*
> —1 PETER 5:7

One reason for anxiety is disbelief and mistrust. Why don't we trust? Because trusting means relinquishing *control,* giving power over to another. At that moment we are exposed and vulnerable to the uncontrollable. Exposure means weakness to us and we cannot stand to be weak in any sense. We seek to maintain control of the known thinking we will be strong.

Jesus says just the opposite: "In weakness we are made strong." We were never designed to carry the burdens of life as we try to do. Anxiety is, in a way, our short-circuiting under the burden that we are attempting to carry. Anxiety is a constant reminder that we are not as strong as we would like to think. When you realize that you do not need to be in control, that people can be trusted to some degree, and that God can be trusted totally, your anxiety will begin to subside. When we take control, we lose control. When we relinquish control to God, we receive the power we desire.

Lord, help me give up my need to control.

*For if anyone thinks himself to be something, when
he is nothing, he deceives himself. But let each one
examine his own work, and then he will have
rejoicing in himself alone, and not in another.
For each one shall bear his own load.*

—GAL. 6:3–5

Greg was sitting at the Wednesday board meeting
when it hit him. Old business must be resolved before
new business! Why had he fought this part of his recovery so long?

In his recovery group they had been talking about
Step Four: "made a searching and fearless moral inventory of ourselves." Although he had given God control of his addiction to work he wanted to put the past
behind him. But now it suddenly made sense: to move
to the new you must first face the old.

That night he began to remember his relationship
with his father. They had a distant relationship primarily because his father worked hard as a laborer to get
ahead but never had time it seemed to spend time with
him. He had vowed as a child never to work as hard as
his father. Now he realized that he needed to admit and
face his unmet dependency needs.

Father, give me the courage to face my past hunger for love.

He who regards reproof will be honored.
—PROV. 13:18

Greg was now feeling guilty and sad about his relationship with his son. He was thinking about that innocent vow he made as a child to make more money so he could spend more time with his family than his father had spent with him. A closer examination revealed it was no better.

Greg realized that he wanted a close relationship with his son but he didn't know how to have one.

Often our unmet dependency needs from the past get converted into behaviors in the present that we believe will resolve our problems. This is what drives our compulsions and fails to meet these needs.

After realizing this, Greg began to pray about his erroneous thoughts and ways and committed to God a desire to rectify his relationships. The first place he confessed this publicly was in his support group. He had a great sense of relief knowing that he was accepted by the other group members.

Consider how your relationships from the past compare to those in your present life. Ask God to cleanse you of any impure motives.

*Command those who are rich in this present age
not to be haughty, nor to trust in uncertain riches
but in the living God, who gives us richly all things
to enjoy.* —1 TIM. 6:17

The story is told about a protegé of the famous steel magnate Andrew Carnegie. He wired his boss one day, excited about the previous day's business. "All records broken yesterday," the telegram said. Expecting congratulations, he was taken aback when the response from Carnegie simply said, "What have you done today?" Carnegie was teaching him the lesson that he could not rest on his laurels if he expected to succeed in life. He has a good point—to a degree.

This attitude is the basis for workaholism. What originally is viewed as the goal toward success ultimately turns into tyranny. Can you imagine what it would be like for the players if the coach of this year's Super Bowl champions received the trophy, canceled the celebration, and called for a practice the next morning?

The Scriptures speak frequently regarding the enjoyment of our labors and accomplishments. In fact, remembering past accomplishments of God is a key element of worship and a source of encouragement to continue on.

Enjoy your accomplishments—why else do you labor?

July 4 – KEEPING PERSPECTIVE

> *If a man begets a hundred children and lives many years, so that the days of his years are many, but his soul is not satisfied with goodness, or indeed he has no burial, I say that a stillborn child is better than he.*
>
> —ECCL. 6:3

When you coming home, Dad?" The question is from a song by the late Harry Chapin. He tells the story of a father and son's relationship over their lifespan. The father is too busy for the boy, always promising to get together when he comes home: then, they'll "have a good time." When he retires, he wants to reconnect with his grown son. The son, having learned his lesson well from his dad, replies to his father's "When you coming home?" by saying he doesn't know, but they'll "get together then."

It is a powerful song with a sobering message. The song was played once for some executives at a seminar. Many of them wept openly, realizing the song was describing them. What a graphic example of the residue of workaholism!

Think about the energy you are investing in this day. How are you spending it? Today's verse is a sober reminder to keep life in proper perspective. If we have the opportunity to live to an old age may we look back with few regrets.

If we lose perspective, we lose.

He who heeds reproof gets understanding.
—PROV. 15:32

Alan was frustrated in his desire to do the personal inventory part of his recovery. The problem was, he couldn't remember many details of his childhood before the age of fourteen. I told him that what he didn't know gave him as much information as what he did know. We then constructed a genogram of his immediate family as well as his family of origin. A genogram is a family tree that includes as much information as possible about who people are and what kind of relationships they have had in the family.

Usually if we suffer from a work addiction we will discover relatives with addictive or codependent traits throughout the family tree. Alan began this process realizing that there was much he didn't know or never thought to ask. More important, he realized how distant he was from his extended family.

Over the next several months we began to strategize ways in which he might consider making contact with members of his family to reestablish relationships. Alan was frightened by this, initially assuming he would be rejected. However, he was able to look up a cousin and an aunt who were very excited to see him.

_____

Lord, guide me through my family maze to those areas where you have important lessons for me.

> *A word fitly spoken is like apples of gold*
> *In settings of silver.*   —PROV. 25:11

William Arthur Ward is quoted in the *Fort Worth Star-Telegram:* "Flatter me, and I may not believe you. Criticize me and I may not like you. Ignore me, and I may not forgive you. Encourage me, and I will not forget you." Pause for a moment and think about your favorite teacher as a child. Why was he so special? Do you remember encouraging words, spoken by either a friend or adult? How about recently—have you been recognized for any qualities that are not related to performance?

The phrase "apples of gold in settings of silver" has raised questions of meaning for ages. Some say that it means Golden Delicious apples in a silver bowl, a delicacy of sweetness in Hebrew times. Others claim it represents an actual gold ornamental apple in a silver frame, apparently a decoration quite familiar to the people of the time. Either way it represented something that was quite pleasing to the eye. The word of encouragement spoken has the same sensory effect on the ear. Are you providing those unforgettable memories for others? Are you cultivating the remembrance of your own?

Encourage me, Lord, I will not forget you.

"For this reason a man shall leave his father and mother and be joined to his wife, and the two shall become one flesh."
　　　　　　　　　　　　　—EPH. 5:31

The traditional vows read like this: ". . . for richer, for poorer; in sickness and in health. . . ." But the workaholic asks, "Who has time to be sick, or to do much else, for that matter?"

Peter was like that. He loved his wife, but you could not measure it by the amount of time he spent with her. He had not made her a golf widow, nor did he abandon her for the TV during football season.

What he did was work. He liked his job, but that was not why he worked. He worked ten-hour days and many Saturdays because that is what he had seen his parents do. To him, long hours at the office did not mean he didn't love his wife. But that was the message she heard.

Peter had been married for four years but he had not yet left home. He did not call Mom and Dad every week and they did not check up on him, either. But he kept a lifestyle that was accepted in his family of origin but was damaging his own family.

Have you left everything you needed to leave from your old family? What message do your actions send to your mate?

> *"And if your hand makes you sin, cut it off. It is*
> *better for you to enter into life maimed, than*
> *having two hands, to go to hell."*
> —MARK 9:43

Believe it or not, the Internal Revenue Service has an account set up to receive payments from citizens who, for one reason or another, send the government money voluntarily. It is called, among other things, the guilt fund. Each year the IRS receives thousands of dollars from many people. The primary reason people send the money is to pay the tax that they had successfully evaded.

I have often wondered what motivated people to pay taxes after successfully evading them. A hint may be found in Step Nine of the Twelve Step program: "Made direct amends to such people whenever possible, except when to do so would injure them or others." I wonder how many recovering addicts have taken this step so seriously that they make amends to even the impersonal government. We have to admire their determination to make amends. I wonder how concerned we are about keeping a clear conscience. What price are we willing to pay to bring about recovery in our own lives?

Lord, please give us the courage to face those whom we have offended, that we might be healed.

*"And the tax collector, standing afar off, would not
so much as raise his eyes to heaven, but beat his
breast, saying, 'God, be merciful to me a sinner!'"*
—LUKE 18:13

When you care enough to send the very best." All of
us are familiar with Hallmark cards and their standard
of excellence.

Often we are not satisfied unless we have done the
very best. I frequently hear, "If it is not worth doing
right, then it is not worth doing at all." The principle is
healthy when applied with balance and perspective.
Unfortunately, most perfectionists know little about
balance and perspective. It is difficult to know the
point at which the "best" becomes the "very best."

Read the two verses preceding today's verse. They
speak of a religious leader who considered himself in
the "very best" category. His accomplishments were
indeed very good, but not good enough for God.

The tax collector knew his works would not satisfy
God, so he asked for mercy. The religious leader
thought his works would satisfy God, and he became
prideful about it.

The religious man did do better things than the tax
collector, but he still needed the same kind of mercy.
His "very best" was still not good enough.

Do you need mercy, or do you think your best is good enough?

> *Though he fall, he shall not be utterly cast down;*
> *For the LORD upholds him with His hand.*
> —PS. 37:24

Cassie was dangerously close to suicide the first time I saw her for an appointment. She was convinced there was no reason for living. I asked why, and she shared how she had strived her entire Christian life to be perfect. The more she talked the angrier she became. Cassie was angry because God didn't deliver! Cassie had been sexually abused by her father. Her anger and fear turned into sexual acting out during her teen years. She did all this to numb her inner hunger for love.

Now Cassie was mad at God because the Christian husband he had given her was insensitive and cold. She expected him to be all the things her father wasn't. To make matters worse, her husband was a workaholic and a perfectionist—not the man of her dreams who would fill her need for love.

Some counseling she had received led her to believe she had to perform by God's perfect standards or be condemned. This experience paralleled her experience as a child and triggered her depression.

Trust God to guide your steps instead of molding yourself to fit a perceived standard.

Cast your burden on the LORD,
And He shall sustain you.
—PS. 55:22

Cassie wanted me to give her a bunch of rules for her to conform to so she could prove how unlovable she was. I shared my belief that no matter how terrible a person she was, God still loved her.

Cassie was a performance-oriented Christian. She believed she had to work her way to God's love. Her earliest recollection of childhood was being told by her mother that she was a mistake. Her father added to this by sexually abusing her. As the oldest child in her family she always worked hard, hoping if she was "good enough" things would change. As an adult, Cassie put God and her husband in the same category as her father and expected abuse. She even expected and tried every trick she knew to get them to reject her.

When they didn't, she began to talk about death less and became open to living. My only instruction to her during this time was to reduce her level of performance to only those things that satisfied her.

We must cast our anxiety on God and trust him for our needs.

I was so foolish and ignorant;
I was like a beast before You.
Nevertheless I am continually with You;
You hold me by my right hand.
—PS. 73:22–23

Billy was the regional real estate sales leader in only his second year of business. He *loves* selling real estate. In a way, a person who loves his work as much as Billy is to be envied. But Billy had made a mistake. "He left his headlights on," as our psychiatrist explained.

Billy had overworked his system to the point of depression and anxiety. He ignored his body's signs that he was fatigued until he had a panic attack while driving. Now he was constantly afraid he would have a panic attack and lose control.

The psychiatrist said that, like a car, Billy's batteries had run down and his brain needed to recharge. He would have to go on medication and change his work habits. He would also have to work on overcoming the psychological fear of recurring panic attacks. Thank God that God is with us even when we ignorantly make mistakes.

Lord, thank you for your mercy, wisdom, and healings!

> *"The servant therefore fell down before him,*
> *saying, 'Master, have patience with me, and*
> *I will pay you all.'"*
> —MATT. 18:26

Greg had a Ph.D., but his common sense and integrity left much to be desired. He moved out of his home and left his wife and children. For about a year he lived like a bachelor, dating often and sleeping with two or three different women a month.

Eventually he realized what he was throwing away and asked to come back. He had married a woman who was willing for him to return. Connie still felt tremendous pain, but she believed it was the right thing to do.

His remorse was real, but he thought he could repay God and his wife for the way he had treated her. And she agreed.

I asked them to get a calculator and look at Matthew 18:21–34. If you are interested you can do your own figuring, but basically the slave owed about ten million dollars and the average income then was eighteen cents a day.

Connie could forgive Greg, but he could not repay God or her. He could only do what was right from here on.

Are you trying to repay a debt you cannot repay, or are you waiting for a repayment that can never come? Forgiveness is not scorekeeping.

> *In the beginning God created the heavens and the earth.*
> —GEN. 1:1

In the book *We Are Driven* one of the recovery suggestions is to assess where you have an opportunity to use your creative talents. When we are driven by work, one way to break free of the mold is to develop hobbies or crafts that take our mind off more serious matters. This can only work if it is something fun and relaxing and not another compulsion.

When taking an inventory of your creative pursuits list some from each of two groups. The first includes things you enjoy doing on your own; the second includes creative pursuits your spouse or the whole family will enjoy. If you fail to do this your family will suffer from your lack of attention. When you do find activities for them to participate in creatively, be sure to let them be creative. Keep that perfectionist in you quiet. Children develop positive self-images by using their own ideas. If your kids help you plant flowers and they plant one crooked, don't fix it!

Since we are created in God's image, don't you think he enjoys when we use the imaginative part of our being?

You are of God, little children, and have overcome
them, because He who is in you is greater than he
who is in the world. —1 JOHN 4:4

The second step of the Twelve Step program is "Came
to believe that a Power greater than ourselves could
restore us to sanity." The popular concept of insanity is
a picture of a disheveled person in a straightjacket,
huddled in the corner of his padded cell, babbling gib-
berish.

Sanity is really a derivative of the Latin *sanitat,* from
which we get the word *sanitary.* It simply means
"health." Any form of addiction—be it drug, alcohol,
sex, food, relationships, gambling, or work—is characterized by an imbalance of perspective. And that is not
healthy. Recognizing that imbalance and admitting
you are not healthy is the first step to recovery. But it is
not enough.

The key to recovery from any habit or addiction is to
recognize there is a personal, caring, involved God
who is *very* interested in helping us recover. But what a
comfort it is to realize that God is here to help us!

Lord, help us to remember that you are not simply a Higher Power
but are personally involved with us.

> *When all that generation had been gathered to*
> *their fathers, another generation arose after them*
> *who did not know the LORD nor the work which He*
> *had done for Israel.* —JUDG. 2:10

Joshua had just died and been buried in the two verses preceding today's. Joshua was a brilliant field general who replaced Moses as the leader of the nation of Israel. The book that bears his name is full of stories of his military conquests and accomplishments.

He was well trained and rich in achievement. He had received on-the-job instruction from Moses for forty years. He had seen the miracles that had propelled the Israelites out of Egypt. He had been one of only twelve chosen to spy in the promised land. He had motivated an entire nation to great accomplishments.

But when he died, there was no one to take his place. He lived an outstanding life and left no heritage. He had been trained by Moses. Whom had he trained? Where were his sons to take up his cause? There is not even a mention of the children of Joshua.

What kind of legacy and heritage do you want to leave behind? What are you doing now to ensure it will happen?

*Now this is the confidence that we have in Him,
that if we ask anything according to His will, He
hears us. And if we know that He hears us,
whatever we ask, we know that we have the
petitions that we have asked of Him.*
—1 JOHN 5:14–15

Barry's father was a rageaholic who was known in
the neighborhood as the "volcano." Barry dodged the
verbal "lava" his father would spew by being a hard-
working martyr. Barry had instincts so finely tuned to
his father's moods he could predict his rages in advance. If he sensed danger he would immediately go
ask his father if there was any work he could help him
with around the house. This frequently would prevent
his father's outburst and his dad would give him some
task to do.

Barry was determined to give his family a better life.
He enjoyed his time with them but struggled with his
inability to leave the office on time. It finally occurred
to him that there was a connection between his workaholism and his childhood. Barry realized that, as a
child, he spent so much energy avoiding pain he never
got his needs met. Even now whenever he felt insecure
he had to work just like he did as a child when he expected his father to erupt.

---

*Barry was astonished to learn that his heavenly Father would not go
into a rage if he humbly made a request. Ask him today for what you
need.*

Even the youths shall faint and be weary,
And the young men shall utterly fall.
—ISA. 40:30

I had forgotten how to relax," reflected Lauren as she described her recent second honeymoon in the Caribbean. A fellow therapist, she could identify the dynamics she was experiencing. She and her husband wanted the trip to be special. They both held stressful jobs in the inner city and the contrast of the tropical sun in the islands was exactly what they needed to recuperate. But two days into the retreat Lauren found herself grumpy and irritable. It was difficult to do nothing and she found herself pacing the beach and thinking of her work. With determination she made herself relax, as strange as it sounds, and she did have a good time after all.

Lauren had to use some old relaxation skills that had been neglected. She came back determined to use them regularly.

Many of these skills are learned in childhood and they never leave us. Rediscover your favorite childhood way to relax. Did you like to play ball? Find a sport and get involved. Reread some of your favorite stories; watch some of your favorite movies.

Remember to practice relaxing.

*Rest in the L*ORD*, and wait patiently for Him;*
Do not fret because of him who prospers in his
  way,
Because of the man who brings wicked schemes
  to pass.
                                    —PS. 37:7

By his mid-twenties Chris was already making more money than his physician father had. He and his wife lived in a near-mansion that was well within their means, and he was not even close to peaking.

But Chris had a score to settle. He had been burned and he liked to see old debts paid back quickly. Years before, he had paid his dues under a supervisor who had no integrity. Chris had been deceived and manipulated but was now in a position to even the score. The only thing that made him hesitate was the possibility that his actions would make him just as ugly as his former supervisor.

He was a young believer in Jesus Christ and came to talk about the conflict inside him. It was foreign to his way of thinking to wait and let God deal out justice, but Chris decided he had nothing to lose.

So he waited, and he has continued to do so for more than two years. Nothing devastating has happened to the supervisor. But a transformation has taken place in Chris. He is no longer eaten up with the need to get even.

———————

Lord, help me to wait on you and let you do what you know is best in me and in the one who has hurt me.

No one engaged in warfare entangles himself with the affairs of this life, that he may please him who enlisted him as a soldier.
—2 TIM. 2:4

When we think of boundaries we typically think of property lines that are marked by roads, signs, or fences. But boundaries in our personal lives are much more subjective.

While driving to work one day I saw a building that had a foundation with the wooden studding up, but no sides, doors, windows, or roof. I also drove past a prison with high barbed-wire fences and bars on all the windows.

Each of these represents unhealthy personal boundaries. The new partially completed home is like a fragmented boundary in our lives. Imagine living in it. The absence of walls, doors, and roof leaves you totally exposed to the elements. To maintain boundaries at work that aren't fragmented we have to say no and set clear limits.

The prison goes to the other extreme and represents a rigid boundary. No one gets in, no one gets out. You are very secure with this kind of boundary but cut off from the rest of the world.

———

Ask God to help you only let in the good things so that his victory in you may be complete.

"He has sent Me . . .
To give them beauty for ashes."
—ISA. 61:1, 3

Americans waited nervously during the reentry of the space shuttle on its maiden flight into space. It was a time when the shuttle would undergo extensive stress. The craft could break up because it could not be pretested to determine if it was structurally adequate.

The thought of the shuttle came to mind as I spoke with Lynn, who was contemplating reentry into the workplace. She had overextended herself as a bank manager and consequently had suffered exhaustion, depression, and anxiety. She went on disability and came for therapy as part of her recovery. She had learned in counseling to set new boundaries, but only in theory. Like the shuttle, there was only one way to find out if the job was done correctly. She went back to work. She went back with the experience and knowledge of how not to do it—and why. Her failures ultimately made her a better person.

Isn't it wonderful to consider this verse in light of all our failures? God wants us to understand that he is powerful enough to bring good out of the worst of situations.

————

There is always hope when God is involved.

> *But God has chosen the foolish things of the world*
> *to put to shame the wise, and God has chosen the*
> *weak things of the world to put to shame the things*
> *which are mighty.*
> —1 COR. 1:27

When Bill Wilson drafted the twelve steps to recovery that are the backbone of the Alcoholics Anonymous program, he chose as the first step the following: "We admitted that we were powerless over alcohol, that our lives had become unmanageable." He recognized the need to deal with the first blockade of resistance to recovery—the issue of power and control. Admitting the loss of control is the first step to regaining control. By denying our powerlessness we expend a great deal of energy. The use of so much energy prohibits us from resting, and the lack of rest further increases the loss of control. When we admit that we are wasting energy trying to control our unmanageable lives, we are able to relax and our burden is lifted.

We must learn to rely on God to do his perfect work, even when it seems to contradict the "experts." Meditate on the paradox of this verse today. You may be empowered as never before.

He that loses his life shall find it.

*"Behold, I send the Promise of My Father upon you;
but tarry in the city of Jerusalem until you are
endued with power from on high."*

—LUKE 24:49

All this talk about workaholism, perfectionism, and obsessions can result in discouragement. Even in this devotional we have addressed the issue as a disease, a tendency, a struggle, and a battle.

There is also the very distinct possibility that you have read these pages so far and have seen nothing new to you. You have known the insatiable nature of perfectionism. You have felt the tug-of-war between being at the office and being at home. You have been on the losing side of an obsession. You may be screaming, "Stop telling me what to do and tell me how to do it!"

Fair enough. Look at today's verse. Jesus had just spent three years telling his disciples what they should do. He had modeled for them everything they would need in the future. Just because their education was complete did not mean they were ready. He told them not to do anything until they were empowered.

The same truth applies to you. You need power to deal with your addictions. What is the source of your power? Is it "from on high" or from within?

> *Whoever has no rule over his own spirit*
> *Is like a city broken down, without walls.*
> —PROV. 25:28

Charlene was a gifted academician who was a senior research assistant at a large university. She had a B.S.N., M.S.N., M.P.H., and was currently working on her third master's degree. At the moment she was devastated because the relationship she thought would lead to marriage had broken up.

"Why does this always happen to me? I get a solid relationship with a guy, we get engaged, and then he breaks it off." This was the third time this had happened to Charlene and she didn't have a clue.

At first I didn't know why, but due to her codependent family history I suspected an addiction. She worked normal hours and didn't drink or use drugs, but she did admit to compulsive eating when not in a relationship with a man.

I asked Charlene how the men in her life felt about her ambition. She quickly responded that they all initially were attracted by it. But when I looked closer at her file I noticed a correlation between the dates of her engagements and the dates she started new master's programs.

Charlene was still in denial about a compulsion to work on more education. Ask God to reveal to you all of your compulsive behaviors.

He who loves silver will not be satisfied with silver;
Nor he who loves abundance, with increase.
This also is vanity.
—ECCL. 5:10

Charles Spurgeon, a great preacher during the last century, used to warn his divinity students of the allure of wealth and how detrimental it was to their ministry. He said, "If you want riches, put it the furthest goal from you." There is a paradox here that is also found in Scripture. The paradox is that things are not what they appear, but often are just the opposite from what we would think.

We've all heard the story of Midas and his touch of gold. If you recall, Midas wanted great wealth and Silenus granted him that wish by causing everything he touched to turn into gold. He was exuberant at first, but he soon found himself in bondage to his desire. The climax of the story came when he longed to touch the most precious thing in his life—his daughter. He did, and she turned to gold. He got what he asked for.

Let us try to remember the fable of Midas as well as this verse today. Do you really believe what Spurgeon said? Do you believe that if you maintain your integrity you will have fulfillment in life?

Lord, help us resist the desire of Midas.

> *"The accuser of our brethren . . . accused them
> before our God day and night."* —REV. 12:10

Though Maria was well educated, handled her money wisely, and had many friends, she still beat up on herself.

She eventually became depressed from trying to carry the load. Her ability to function became impaired, her fatigue rose sharply, and she lost control of her weight.

Her recent failures had proven to Maria that she should be disappointed with herself. It was a self-perpetuating downward spiral. To deal with the crisis we first had to identify her "gaps." At first she thought I was referring to her inability to perform. Not so.

Imagine two horizontal lines. The line on top represents total health, the one on bottom stands for complete depravity. In reality Maria was somewhere between the two.

But she was looking at only one gap. She was measuring only the distance from where she was to the top line—where she wanted to be. She was ignoring the distance between where she was and the bottom line—where she had come from. Her accuser constantly reminded her of the "accusation gap." She neglected to notice the "praise gap."

Which gap do you review the most often?

And I thank Christ Jesus our Lord who has enabled me, because He counted me faithful, putting me into the ministry.
　　　　　　　　　　　　　—1 TIM. 1:12

Scott was smiling as he shared with me what God was doing in his life. I hadn't seen Scott, a corporate executive, in over a year. When I last saw him he was well on his way to recovery from his work addiction.

Scott went on to share that he had made a career change. It began when Scott shared his experience with others at his office who became curious and began asking for help for themselves. This grew into a small support group, which emphasized balanced living in Christ and offered prayer and support.

The group continued to grow, and within six months they needed a larger room to accommodate everyone. Then one day after one of their meetings an older man said, "Scott, wouldn't it be something if we had an organization that could meet the needs of people who suffer from work addiction so that we could reach more people with God's message?" Scott told me God planted that seed in his heart, and now he was starting that organization.

When God heals you he often calls you into his service to reach out to others. Pray for his guidance in this area.

For thus says the Lord God, the Holy One of Israel:

> *"In returning and rest you shall*
>   *be saved;*
> *In quietness and confidence shall*
>   *be your strength."*
> *But you would not.*

—ISA. 30:15

Carly Simon sang a popular song in the seventies that contained the phrase, "but I haven't got time for the pain." This verse could be considered the theme song of the workaholic. Workaholics work to avoid pain. The pain may emanate from the past, such as constant criticism from a parent. The pain may come from a present source of suffering, such as a problem marriage. We can either face the pain or deny it, but we can never avoid it. I once asked a client who had been experiencing severe abdominal pain why he had not gone to the doctor. His answer was typical: "I don't want to receive any bad news."

Imagine driving in your car and the alternator light goes on. You pull off the road, reach under the dash, and pull the wire out. The light goes off and you drive merrily on your way. Ridiculous as it sounds, workaholics do the same thing by trying to numb their pain with work. The remedy that God has in mind is much simpler: be still, face the pain, know that he is in control of all our situations.

Lord, help us to be still and have the courage to let you work.

> *"'You shall love the LORD your God with all your heart, with all your soul, and with all your mind.' This is the first and great commandment. And the second is like it: 'You shall love your neighbor as yourself.'"*
> —MATT. 22:37–39

The religious leaders of Jesus' day must have been accountants. They were always interested in the bottom line. Jesus revealed the top two commandments in response to a question from one of those leaders.

We are not so different today. We are still interested in the bottom line. Jesus did not tell the questioner that his was an inappropriate question. In fact, the ruler only asked for the top commandment. Jesus gave number one and number two. He obviously thought both were worthy of his comment.

Jesus said that life boils down to relationships—specifically, three interpersonal relationships. One, relationship with God; two, relationship with other people; three, relationship with self.

I find that people who come in for therapy have only one or two of these relationships in functional condition.

Do a quick spot check. Which of those three in your life is healthiest? Which of the three needs the most attention? Are any of the three lifeless? Get help if you need it.

Hear my cry, O God;
Attend to my prayer.
From the end of the earth I will cry to You,
When my heart is overwhelmed;
Lead me to the rock that is higher than I.
—PS. 61:1–2

Eddie was a baggage handler for a major airline. He grew up with an alcoholic father who frequently would go into rages. Eddie was much more laid back and had a strong commitment to his wife. However, they had fought frequently about his long absences due to his working overtime.

One day he came home to discover his wife in tears. She said that out of loneliness she had begun to see another man in the neighborhood. She said she never dreamed it would happen, but they had gone to bed together.

Eddie and his wife immediately got counseling to reconcile this unexpected scar on their marriage. Eddie was convicted by his addiction to work and his desire to provide a good home for his wife. He already believed in God but now decided to turn his life over to him completely.

God, I have botched up my life without you; please take control and have mercy.

When you sit down to eat with a ruler,
Consider carefully what is before you;
And put a knife to your throat
If you are a man given to appetite.
　　　　　　　　　—PROV. 23:1–2

A hunter returned from the field with his game and happened upon a fisherman who was walking home with his catch of fish. Each stopped to admire the other's take and soon found himself wishing for the other's food, so they traded. This continued day after day until they each began to desire to keep what they had. They had become sick and tired of what originally had been a novel exchange. The moral of the story was "abstain and enjoy."

This was the essence of one of Aesop's fables that I had been reading with my nine-year-old daughter. What caught my attention was that peculiar moral. It seemed to be a contradiction of sorts. How can you enjoy something you abstain from? It finally dawned on me that self-discipline is often its own reward. A great deal of satisfaction and increased self-esteem come from saying no to a negative temptation. It is just as important to learn to resist the positive temptations such as overwork, overservice, and overcleanliness.

Practice overcoming the compulsion to do; sit back and enjoy the victory you have earned.

> *Like newborn babes, long for the pure milk of the word, that by it you may grow in respect to salvation.*
> —1 PETER 2:2, NAS

The process of dealing with workaholism or perfectionism follows the same principles as the Twelve Step program used by alcoholics to overcome their addiction. The reason is that the workaholic and the perfectionist are a different sort of addict. They do not succumb to a drug, but they do become controlled by an external entity.

To address our relationship to ourselves, the attention is actually the same as in Step One of the Twelve Step program: admitting powerlessness over addictions and admitting an unmanageable life.

I have a two-year-old son. His view of life is marked by joy, freedom, impulsiveness and no thought for tomorrow. On the other hand, when his nose runs, someone else has to wipe it. He has no ability to govern his own needs. He is messy and easily embarrassed, and he does not yet know much about pride.

Is it difficult for you to admit that you need "your nose wiped," so to speak? Until an adult admits he needs help he cannot receive it. Do you need help? Become like a little child. They need others to help them.

Two are better than one,
Because they have a good reward for their labor.
For if they fall, one will lift up his companion.
But woe to him who is alone when he falls,
For he has no one to help him up.

—ECCL. 4:9–10

Bill told Joe about a fight he and Kathy had the evening before. Kathy was upset because Bill had stayed late at the office twice the week before. Bill was completing a project for which there were high penalties for not meeting the deadline.

Joe asked Bill questions to see if the story he gave Kathy was valid. In this case it was only a half-truth. Bill hadn't mentioned that during the contract negotiation he did not share with his boss his feelings that they would be pushing too hard. Bill knew the price to pay would be personal time. Bill had let his need to please the boss get in the way of his instincts.

Joe helped Bill identify this and get back on track by being honest with both his wife and his boss. Having a non-related buddy or prayer partner is critical to maintenance.

Do you have a same-sex friend to confide in who will hold you accountable for your recovery?

> *"But they refused to heed, shrugged their shoulders,*
> *and stopped their ears so that they could not hear."*
> —ZECH. 7:11

Andy and Jane had a problem; his name was Jason and he was twelve years old. Jason was a gifted child, yet his report card didn't show it. Jane was convinced that Andy was a primary reason why Jason was doing so poorly. It was not because Andy berated Jason and made him feel inferior. The problem was that Andy was seldom home. For the past two years he had poured himself into the new business he had started. He was gone on Saturdays, he would stay late long after the children had gone to bed, and he would even pull some all-nighters occasionally.

Andy did not see the connection between his actions and Jason's. Instead he rationalized by saying, "I was just like Jason at his age—he'll get over it." He was in pure denial.

I'm not sure how it is going to turn out. I felt the same sensations talking to Andy that I feel when I try to discuss an alcoholic's addiction with him. You may have been where Andy is. Aren't you glad that you responded to the tug of God and loved ones?

Lord, help us not to slip into darkness after we have felt the light.

He is the image of the invisible God, the firstborn
over all creation.
                                        —COL. 1:15

I do not know what you think about spiritual things in general or about Jesus in particular. But I assume you agree that he lived the most unique life anyone ever has.

Consider the following. He never traveled more than one hundred miles from where he was born. He never wrote a book. He never had more than five hundred followers in his lifetime. He lived in an obscure area of the world, far distant from the power centers of that day. His public life lasted only three years. He was a member of a despised race. He died as a common criminal. Upon his death all his followers scattered and hid.

And yet more space is devoted to him in the encyclopedia than to George Washington, Abraham Lincoln, and Thomas Jefferson combined. The date we write every day is based on the year in which he was born. Principles of governments are based upon his teachings.

———————

Do you know who he was, or is? If Step One is true and we are power-less and this man is powerful, it stands to reason we should learn more about him.

"And behold, I am coming quickly, and My reward is with Me, to give to every one according to his work. I am the Alpha and the Omega, the Beginning and the End, the First and the Last."
—REV. 22:12–13

In their book *We Are Driven*, Hemfelt, Minirth, and Meier discuss the concept of learning to "suspend time through God." They point out that workaholics have a tendency to focus only on chronological time. This drives us to keep track or set goals only in this dimension of time. For example, we might ask ourselves, "How many sales calls did I make today?" or "How far must I drive before I rest?"

These questions drive us to our addictive behaviors. The authors suggest that this causes us to pick up our pace and ultimately fail. We need to understand that our life is limited and we need to enjoy the quality of it. As we get closer to Christ we begin to experience a greater sense of peace and the quality the authors refer to as "time standing still."

Christ's words in today's text remind us that he is the beginning and the end of all time, and we can rest in that comfort.

A dear friend once said, "All things in this life will pass, only what's done for Christ will last."

I press toward the goal for the prize of the upward call of God in Christ Jesus. —PHIL. 3:14

Rod is a recovering workaholic. He had been a pastor who worked incessantly to be a "champion for God." He had been challenged by his mentor, a successful pastor, to work eighteen hours a day. The mentor used an Olympic champion as an example: "If an athlete could commit himself totally to attain a medal, the man of God should labor even more for the cause of Christ." For all that Christ gave for him could he give any less than his all?

There is much truth to this reasoning. We do owe Christ our all and we honor him by doing our best. But Rod was motivated by guilt and competition. Also, he overlooked one other important point in the champion analogy: Olympians train intensely for only a short period of their lives. Rod expected to pour it on forever. Rod had to burn out and be hospitalized before he realized that he could not become a champion for God on his own schedule.

The Lord wants us to pace ourselves by keeping all areas of our lives in balance. Learn to say to yourself, "Be patient—God is."

Lord, teach us to be patient while you do your work.

> *"I and My Father are one." . . . The Jews answered*
> *Him, saying, "For a good work we do not stone*
> *You, but for blasphemy, and because You, being a*
> *Man, make Yourself God."* —JOHN 10:30, 33

Jesus said he was God. If I need power then Jesus would be a source for me. Right? Only if he told the truth. So he says he is God. Even though his enemies, the Jews, heard him say that, that still does not make it true. How can I know it's true?

Most people like the things Jesus said, did, and represented as he walked on the earth. Usually, if they do not want to deal with the deity question, they say he was a good, moral teacher, and that if I would just do some of the things he said my life would be better for it. But he did not leave us that option.

C. S. Lewis, the British philosopher, had an interesting way of thinking about this claim to deity. He said for a person to claim to be God there are only three possible explanations. One, he was not God and knew he was not God. Two, he was not God but sincerely thought he was God. Three, he was God. In short, Jesus leaves us to choose whether he was a liar, a lunatic, or Lord.

Who is this Jesus to you? If you need power you need to do something with him.

> *"My grace is sufficient for you, for My strength is made perfect in weakness." Therefore most gladly I will rather boast in my infirmities, that the power of Christ may rest upon me.* —2 COR. 12:9

I never fail to be amazed at how much power there is in weakness. It is such a simple principle of God's creation, yet those suffering from addictions do not understand it.

If I give my weak body a good night's sleep I rise renewed. If I let go of my need to be perfect and confess my weakness, others are attracted to me. I may ask God for something I want many times, but often it is not until I stop asking that I get it.

We begin to experience things like this as we maintain our recovery. We get more balance as we take responsibility for being vulnerable and admitting our weaknesses.

There will be many paradoxes along the way as we learn more about maintaining our balance. One thing is for certain—we can always trust the Lord, who needs our obedience and weaknesses.

Father, I commit to you all my weaknesses so that you may use these things to develop your strength in me.

"But I say to you, love your enemies, bless those who curse you, do good to those who hate you, and pray for those who spitefully use you and persecute you."
—MATT. 5:44

Most Americans know what you are talking about when you use the term "Type A." Friedman and Rosenman, who coined the term, define it as "any person who is aggressively involved in a chronic, incessant struggle to achieve more and more in less and less time, and if required to do so, against the opposing efforts of other things or persons."

Place this definition against the verse for today. What a contrast! The verse describes what we could call the "type C" person, for Christ. The "type A" person is *driven,* and can't relax or resist a challenge. The "type C," on the other hand, is able to *respond* and not react to the environment. What's the difference between the two? I believe "type C" has come to accept the reality that genuine fulfillment is beyond her ability to achieve. She has learned that the sovereignty of God is real in her life. She knows that the self-restraint that this verse calls for does make sense and that the payoff far outweighs the cost of self-denial.

Lord, give us the eyes of faith to see what is best for us.

"Eye has not seen, nor ear heard,
Nor have entered into the heart of man
The things which God has prepared
for those who love Him."

—1 COR. 2:9

When I lived in Africa four of us took a vacation to Victoria Falls. The African name for it translates into "smoke that thunders." That clearly describes the scene.

Surprisingly, the falls are not up in the hills or on the side of a cliff. They are in the center of a broad, flat plain. The Zambesi River drops almost one hundred yards straight down into a mile-long gorge that is only about thirty yards from edge to edge.

The result of this huge river falling straight down is a plume of spray that reaches more than a mile into the sky. When we walked on the opposite side of it we were soaked within seconds.

Dan and I went early one morning to see the falls before the crowds arrived. We sat in our own silence for more than half an hour. The noise was deafening. I could hear nothing but the roar of the water. Later, Dan apologized for singing so loudly as we sat next to each other. I had not heard a note.

Is there any noise in your life that is keeping you from hearing what God has prepared for you?

> *For no other foundation can anyone lay than that*
> *which is laid, which is Jesus Christ.*
> —1 COR. 3:11

Mike knew that to lead a balanced life he had to make decisions and set goals that would enable him to maintain his recovery.

The first and most difficult decision Mike made was to limit the number of hours he spent at the office per week. He decided on forty-five hours maximum and if he went over he would compensate himself the following week.

He also decided not to take business calls at home except for emergencies, and he stopped taking his briefcase home.

When he made these decisions Mike thought he would not be a popular fellow at the office. But in fact, he discovered that he became a more productive and creative manager who was well respected.

Every decision we make in life has either positive or negative consequences. To live a balanced life we must be willing to experience both.

You therefore, beloved, since you know these things beforehand, beware lest you also fall from your own steadfastness, being led away with the error of the wicked. —2 PETER 3:17

Mike decided to share his decision with his boss and those working under him. His boss said he could run his department any way he wanted as long as the work got done.

Next Mike met with his department heads and explained the position he was taking. He said he expected anyone who worked in his department to operate with the same philosophy. He gave workers the option of transferring to another department if they had problems working a time-limited week. A few skeptics made some noise, but everyone stayed.

Slowly others followed his lead in making new decisions and setting new boundaries. Staff came to work more rested and more creative. They began to see solutions that were invisible before. They also set limits on how business was done between departments and made recommendations to work more effectively. The end results surprised the boss so much he offered Mike a promotion.

All things are possible with God. If you maintain your boundaries and make decisions for health you should enjoy your work and play.

Therefore we also, since we are surrounded by so great a cloud of witnesses, let us lay aside every weight, and the sin which so easily ensnares us, and let us run with endurance the race that is set before us.
—HEB. 12:1

Larry Bird recently scored his twenty-thousandth point, making him only the fifth player in NBA history to reach that plateau. The crowd cheered him for the longest time while he was presented with the game ball. He must have known how privileged he was to be the unique recipient of their adulation!

A perceived chorus, or crowd, is always present in the mind of the perfectionist. Unlike Bird's chorus of adoring Celtic fans, the workaholic's chorus is made up of critical, sarcastic images who display disgust at his efforts. There is no satisfaction—only shame. And they are only in the person's imagination.

This Scripture verse speaks of a real chorus of saints who are watching and rooting for us. They know what we are going through because they went through it, too, and came out victorious.

Lord, you are the God of all encouragement. Help us to remember that when the chorus rages against us.

Though I speak with the tongues of men and of angels, but have not love, I have become as sounding brass.
                                                        —1 COR. 13:1

I taught math as a missionary in Africa. My assignment was to teach algebra and introductory calculus to five upper-level classes of thirty-five students each. There were books for almost everyone, each had a desk, everyone came to school, and discipline in the classroom was not a distraction. Aside from the fact that my students had never been taught how to add, subtract, multiply, or divide, I was ready to teach algebra and calculus.

We began with the basics of addition and subtraction, and we made great progress. I thought. The first test I gave them was as easy as I thought possible. No one made better than 33 percent, and the average grade was under 20 percent.

I finally discovered these Africans who spoke British English as a second language could not understand my west Texas drawl. You see, I had learned to talk in Lubbock. And I had not paused to ask if I was being understood.

Are you speaking a language the people in your life cannot understand? Are you speaking with or without love? What message are they hearing from you?

And after the earthquake a fire, but the LORD was
not in the fire; and after the fire a still small voice.
—1 KINGS 19:12

Martha's grandmother kept a perfect home. She never let the dust settle, ironed sheets and underwear, and commanded the other members of the household to follow suit. Martha has been carrying on Grandma's traditions. Although long dead, Grandma still speaks in the still small voice in the back of Martha's head: "Look at this place. It is a filthy mess. What a pig sty!" Keeping house was Grandma's full-time job. Martha has made it her full-time job also—along with working full time, commuting one hour each way, and serving in an official capacity in her church. Mentally, she understands that she is doing far more than Grandma had to, and the stress is far greater as well. Emotionally, though, her understanding has not made much difference.

Martha needs to learn to challenge those sinister whispers that constantly tell her that she should be ashamed of herself. Martha needs to realize that God is also whispering to her. The sinister whispers mercilessly drive us on and God's voice calls for us to relax. If you are not sure which is which, seek counsel.

Be still and know that I am God.

But solid food belongs to those who are of full age,
that is, those who by reason of use have their
senses exercised to discern both good and evil.
—HEB. 5:14

My grandfather taught me how to drive a standard shift car in a green jeep. I was thirteen and the jeep was at least sixteen.

But clutches are a challenge to a novice driver. I knew the basic idea, but my eye-foot-hand coordination was not in gear. I tried to concentrate on where we were headed, watch how fast we were going, and listen to Gramps. Doing more than one of those at the same time was not a possibility.

Gramps was a laid-back, easygoing cowboy. I almost gave up that day, but Gramps would not let me quit. By the end of the day I had at least improved. By week's end it was second nature.

When I had watched him drive the shifting had looked so easy that I expected to do it smoothly on my first try. Only with practice did it become smooth for me.

Such is the case for dealing with perfectionism. Practice is required, but eventually letting go and lowering expectations becomes smooth and natural.

Do you need to practice on any of that?

> *Cause me to hear Your lovingkindness in the*
> *morning,*
> *For in You do I trust;*
> *Cause me to know the way in which I should walk,*
> *For I lift up my soul to You.* —PS. 143:8

Brian was a gifted administrator who worked in a large residential treatment facility for adolescents. He managed the services provided to over eighty teens who came from abusive backgrounds.

On any given day Brian participated in three or four meetings and made decisions about admissions or discharges of residents and the hiring or firing of staff. This facility treated some difficult teenagers, so there were continual crises with residents and high staff turnover. This made Brian's job very unpredictable, requiring long hours and very little rest.

In spite of this Brian enjoyed the work until his wife had a health crisis. He realized his addiction then because he had difficulty pulling away from work. Brian sought treatment and was encouraged that another professional understood his plight.

Lord, help me to find the balance between taking care of the needs in my personal life and doing a good job at work.

Whoever has no rule over his own spirit
Is like a city broken down without walls.
—PROV. 25:28

In doing Brian's inventory we learned that his father had been frequently absent because of his work and had been prone to rages at his family. Brian always swore that he would be more sensitive to the needs of others when he grew up.

It was this revelation that made it possible for Brian to see that he was overidentifying with the people he treated. As a result, he was neglecting his own needs. I recommended that Brian abstain from his job until he could get his life manageable again. In Brian's case this was possible because he had a very liberal leave policy which allowed him to take five weeks off with pay. A few weeks later he felt blessed by his wife's recovery and was tempted to return to work, but he had agreed not to talk about work or go to the office during that month. In the end Brian saw that he needed to change jobs and work with a population he didn't identify with so much.

Has your dedication to your job gotten out of balance?

Surely oppression destroys a wise man's reason.
—ECCL. 7:7

The preacher runs off with the church secretary; the mother abandons her family and acts like a teenager; the upstanding executive blows his brains out. We hear stories like this on a regular basis. We pause and wonder why, then just as quickly shake it off and go about our business, never stopping to think that we might be headed down the same path.

Stress has a peculiar effect on people and it is manifested in many different ways. Prolonged oppression definitely changes the personality. Unless we carefully regulate the stress in our lives it will surely affect us in a negative way. How do we regulate stress? We often do not have control over our circumstances, but we can find ways to offset the stress. The law of physics, "what goes up must come down," applies here. If you have worked hard, find time to play. If life has been giving you a beating, pamper yourself. If you do not learn to regulate yourself, your body will shut down. Constant, unregulated stress will cause you to do things that will hurt you and the ones you love.

Remember the theme of an oil filter commercial: "You can pay me now or you can pay me later."

*For you were bought at a price; therefore glorify
God in your body.*   —1 COR. 6:20

Our Constitution promises us certain rights as citizens of the United States. The Bible also promises certain rights as citizens of the kingdom of God. But we tend to enlarge upon what is actually a "right."

Today's verse indicates that a follower of Jesus Christ has been purchased. Prior to the Civil War, when someone was bought he was called a slave. The same applies here. Believers in Jesus Christ have been bought, and he gives privileges to those who belong to him.

Consider the position of a slave. In reality, a slave has no rights, only responsibilities. Everything a slave may call his own in actuality belongs to his master. For example, as a slave of Jesus Christ, I don't own my time, he does. If someone makes me wait for him, they are not wasting my time because it is no longer mine. If it is not mine, then I have experienced no loss. There is no reason for me to unleash my anger.

Lord, help me to see that all I have is yours, and you give me responsibilities and privileges, not rights. Help me return to you any rights I have taken.

> *I have seen servants on horses,*
> *While princes walk on the ground like servants.*
> —ECCL. 10:7

Chris Zorich was an all-American linebacker for Notre Dame. After the 1990 Orange Bowl, in which he was voted defensive player of the game, Chris phoned home to Chicago to tell his mom he was on his way home. Chris grew up in a rough section of the city. His mother rode her bicycle to work in order to support him. Chris was quoted as saying she was one of the most courageous people he had ever known. She had watched the game as usual and said she looked forward to seeing him. But when Chris arrived home he found her dead in the hallway.

Little is known of Chris Zorich's mother. We know that she endured hardship and raised a son of exemplary character. Solomon noticed that there were noble people who were riding horses who were no more than servants in character. He also noticed those of humble means who were true nobility in character. It sounds like Chris's mother was in the latter category. Let it be a reminder to us as we evaluate what is really important in life.

————————

Lord, give us the wisdom to recognize greatness and follow it.

*I will call upon the LORD, who is worthy to be
   praised;
So shall I be saved from my enemies.*
                              —PS. 18:3

One of the problems faced by American soldiers in
Vietnam was knowing who the enemy was. Children
could be carrying explosives, camp cooks might be
setting booby traps, and old men could be scouts for
the opposite side. It was tough to tell.

Do you know who or what your enemies are? One
of the problems with workaholism, like alcoholism, is
that our enemy wears the outfit of a savior. The very
thing that will suck me in deeper looks like it will lift
me out of the quagmire.

But in the verse there is a comforting thought. It indicates that the Lord is so able and worthy that he will
save me from my enemies. If he will save me from
them then he must be able to identify them! My main
task then becomes only to "call upon the Lord." He will
identify the enemy and direct his troops at the appropriate targets.

One more thought: I am not simply the one saved by
the Lord; I am also one of his soldiers involved in the
battle to save me.

————————

*Lord, you are an accomplished field general and I can rely on your
leadership without reservation.*

> *But if anyone does not provide for his own, and especially for those of his household, he has denied the faith and is worse than an unbeliever.*
> —1 TIM. 5:8

Ginny, the mother of two young daughters, had a compulsion to do volunteer work. Though she wasn't at home much, she rationalized that she just had a "big heart" and liked helping people.

Ginny had training as a nurse, but she and her husband agreed that she needed to be home with the kids while they were small. Ginny started volunteering when her oldest daughter became a Brownie. With Ginny's organizational talents she became troop leader in a few years.

Ginny also developed an interest in her church's Christian education program. She soon volunteered her time to develop curriculum and recruit Sunday school teachers. All of this activity kept Ginny at meetings or on the phone, although she had thought she was working for the benefit of her daughters.

The above verse was convicting because she realized she had failed to meet her daughters' needs. As we discussed her compulsive patterns Ginny became aware of her codependency and was encouraged that change was possible.

Lord, I confess that my well-intended donation of free time was contaminated by something outside my control.

Every wise woman builds her house,
But the foolish pulls it down with her hands.
—PROV. 14:1

Ginny assumed it would be easy to cut back on her volunteer work until she realized she was concerned about what others would think of her. She was so respected by others, and they depended on her so.

She eventually discovered the source of her compulsion as we reviewed her family background. When she was eight her younger sister drowned accidentally. Ginny felt a tremendous amount of guilt for not being able to save her even though the facts said otherwise.

Ginny later was able to see that her volunteerism was a means for her to compensate for the guilt and shame she had buried since childhood. She was able to continue in her recovery and eventually resigned her leadership positions at church and in the community to spend more time with her girls.

Seek God's guidance in exploring your past so you can understand what motivates your drive to work.

> *"And you shall know the truth, and the truth shall make you free."*
> —JOHN 8:32

Philosophers have wrestled with the question for ages and still do: What is truth? The answer, according to Christ, is that he himself is truth and that those who know him now possess the capacity to know truth as well. The knowledge of truth does not come naturally, however. We still tend to distort reality.

As we face the problems of life we must perceive the world around us as accurately as possible. We will never find healing unless we exhibit the courage to face reality. We must stop and examine ourselves and our circumstances on a regular basis. We are often too busy to comprehend what is going on around us.

Truth is presented in Scripture as a hidden treasure; it is only available to those who seek it. The only way to seek it is to devote some time to solving problems and understanding the pain of reality. If we do not attend to these issues in the good times, we will be ill-equipped to handle the difficult times. When was the last time you purposely set time aside and meditated on the truth?

_____

Lord, help us to seek you and know indeed when it is you.

And God is able to make all grace abound toward you, that you, always having all sufficiency in all things, have an abundance for every good work.
—2 COR. 9:8

The tendency of human nature is to depend upon feelings and perceptions more than facts. We give power to our feelings when we believe them, not because they are so forceful in and of themselves.

But the Scriptures tell us that God is able to provide for us an abundance of whatever is necessary to do *every* good deed. Sounds too good to be true, but even that is an indication that we believe our perceptions more than we believe facts.

On this principle Step Two works. Old habit patterns can be so difficult to alter that we believe they will never change. That is where we need to step outside our visible and historical resources and rely on the God who has said he is able.

He has actually put his reputation on the line—he has said he is able. That is either true or it is false. If it is false then there is no hope for any of us. But if it is true then he is responsible to take my trust in him and treat it as an investment.

What have you invested in God recently? I hear he guarantees an unbelievably good return on your investment.

> *So they said, "Believe on the Lord Jesus Christ, and*
> *you will be saved, you and your household."*
> —ACTS 16:31

I like to tell this joke in session: A man goes to the doctor, lifts his elbow, and says, "Doc, it hurts when I do this." The doctor replies, "Don't do that." It illustrates an important point: the answer to a seemingly complex problem is simpler than you may think. Let me give you a real-life example: Jane is an overworked mother of three who is active in ministry, homemaking, and solving the problems of the world. She says she has no time to relax, play, or meditate. Any recommendation to rest is met with a resistant, "I can't." Jane needs to find a way to relax and recuperate.

As a therapist I will try to convince her to relax by using my training to make the simple complex: "There seems to be some intrinsic sociologic transgenerational influence that was embedded in your psyche as a child. It is manifesting itself in the form of a displayed inadequacy that is blocking your teleologic motivation to actualize." The bottom line is, she feels guilty when she relaxes and is not going to overcome the problem until she begins to try.

If it hurts when you work too much—don't work too much!

Then a leper came to Him, imploring Him, kneeling down to Him and saying to Him, "If You are willing, You can make me clean." And Jesus, moved with compassion, put out His hand and touched him, and said to him, "I am willing; be cleansed."

—MARK 1:40–41

This leper must have had an addict somewhere in his family tree, because he was able to live with contradictions. He came to Christ with a tremendous amount of faith and a tremendous amount of doubt.

The diseased man does not doubt that Jesus has the power to wipe clean this man's ugliness. But he hesitates when he questions Jesus' willingness. We do this too. We look at someone who has succeeded in an area and say, "God will do that for him, but he won't do it for me."

There are two crucial points that can slip by unnoticed. First, Jesus does not chastise the man for doubting Jesus' willingness to heal him. It even appears that he responds to the man's honesty. To emphasize his willingness he does the unthinkable: he touches a leper. Second, the phrase "moved with compassion" means quite literally that his stomach tied up in a knot. Jesus was so responsive to the man's cry for help that it affected him physically.

Have you asked Jesus for help lately? He does not chastise for doubts and he is more eager to help than you could ever imagine.

> *Likewise the Spirit also helps in our weaknesses.*
> *For we do not know what we should pray for as*
> *we ought, but the Spirit Himself makes intercession*
> *for us with groanings which cannot be uttered.*
> —ROM. 8:26

Russ knew that his work addiction was less of an in-fluence when he spent his time with other Christians, read his Bible, or prayed. Now that he was working Step Eleven of his Twelve Step program he desired to have an even closer relationship with Christ.

Russ had spent many hours in therapy and had much less difficulty identifying his feelings. I suggested that, when he prayed, he should first imagine getting in touch with his feelings, and then imagine walking up to Jesus and talking about those feelings.

Russ said this made sense, but he often got dis-tracted in prayer. I shared that when this occurs with me, I find it helpful to write my prayer out on paper as if I am writing a letter to Christ. That helps me stay focused and also is a record of my own growth.

Lord, I desire to do your will and to know you more personally.

O Lord, You have searched me and known me. . . .
Such knowledge is too wonderful for me;
It is high, I cannot attain it.   —PS. 139:1, 6

Bill W. recognized self-examination as a key to recovering from addiction. The fourth step of the Twelve Step program says, "Made a searching and fearless moral inventory of ourselves."

There are various reasons why some people overwork. A pastor has a daughter who is terminally ill. His pain is great, yet he does not grieve. Instead, he pours himself into his church and appears even more noble for doing so in the eyes of those around him. He is running from his pain and is hurting his daughter, his wife, and himself.

Do you overwork? Have you stopped long enough to evaluate why? Are you afraid of what you will see? The good news is found in this verse. God already knows us; we cannot surprise him. He is committed to us in spite of our failings. What grace and mercy he shows to us!

———————

Lord, give us the courage to see ourselves as we are and to take an accurate moral inventory.

"If you abide in Me, and My words abide in you,
you will ask what you desire, and it shall be done
for you."
—JOHN 15:7

Leonard and Janet lived in the Middle East. During our visit there we watched oil tankers come and go through the Straits of Hormuz. It was easy to tell which ships were waiting in line to enter the Persian Gulf to take on oil and which were already loaded. The empty ones rode very high on the water; those which were full sank down in the water until only their tops appeared above the surface.

The analogy is that some people are full and apparently useful while other people are empty and obviously wanting. The difference is easily seen, but the remaining question is, "What are you full of?"

Jesus laid down a blank check for us in this verse. To "abide" is to be comfortable. If I become so comfortable with him and his word becomes so comfortable with me, then I can receive what I ask! (I assume that the two-way abiding will affect the things for which I ask.)

Are you comfortable with and full of the life-changing Scripture? Are you making yourself at home with Jesus Christ, the personal God?

*There is an evil which I have seen under the sun,
and it is common among men. . . . God has given
[a man] riches and wealth and honor, so that he
lacks nothing for himself of all he desires; yet God
does not give him power to eat of it.*

—ECCL. 6:1–2

Jack was called the Vacation Buster by his co-workers because of his habit of calling his staff while they were on vacation to conduct business. Jack expected others to be as driven as he was. One day Tony, his most trusted manager, quit abruptly. When Jack called him while he was on a cruise he resigned over the phone and hung up.

Jack reacted by screaming at all his other managers. He didn't remember anything else until he woke up in the hospital with a heart attack.

When the hospital social worker referred him to the clinic we were warned he would be a bear. At first he was, but as we talked he realized that he had scared everyone away. During his long hospital stay he had very few visitors, and he even sensed his family's distance.

Jack was now ready to listen. He knew that he had no control, and he decided to give Christ the reins of his life.

Lord, I want you to take complete control of my life.

> *To the righteous, good shall be repaid.*
> —PROV. 13:21

Jack wanted to reconcile with his co-workers, especially Tony, who had been so loyal. However, Tony refused to answer his phone calls. Jack learned that he was unhappily employed elsewhere but couldn't forgive Jack for ruining his cruise.

When Jack discovered this, he knew what to do. He arranged for an all-expense-paid cruise that was even better than the one Tony and his wife originally went on. Tony refused at first, expecting that some strings were attached, but eventually he accepted the gift.

A year earlier Jack would have hoarded his wealth as a squirrel saves nuts, but he knew God would provide. He was surprised, and cried like a baby, when Tony called him while on the cruise and asked if he could have his old job back.

Making amends can take many forms that may cause some sacrifice. God will most certainly honor your faithfulness through this journey.

Behold, children are a heritage from the LORD,
The fruit of the womb is His reward.

—PS. 127:3

Personalized license plates are really amazing; they reflect the inexhaustible ingenuity of the human mind. My wife and I recently met with our real estate agent, whom we had not seen in some time. Margaret really worked hard to help us find a place to rent when we moved to the Washington, D.C., area. She worked as hard to find us a place to rent as she would have if we were buying a home. So when it came time to buy, we called her. We met her at a model home and immediately noticed the new license plate on her car. Her message was "IM NVRHME." I was afraid to ask why but I did it anyway. Happy-go-lucky as ever, Margaret replied, "That's what my family tells me: 'You're never home, Mom!'"

I promised to give her a copy of this book. I want her to know how appreciative we are of her excellent work ethic and love for people. But I also fear for her family's well-being. Today's verse is a reminder to all of us to keep in perspective the truly important things in life.

Spend time with the matters of long-lasting importance.

> *"But as for you, you meant evil against me; but*
> *God meant it for good, in order to bring it about*
> *as it is this day, to save many people alive."*
> —GEN. 50:20

Inflexibility nags the workaholic and the perfectionist. They usually have a complete picture in their mind as to what should happen.

The small piece of the fabric of life that we can see often seems ill fitting from our perspective. That was Nancy's thinking. Life was not so bad, it was just so different from what she had pictured that she was sure something had to be wrong. She had achieved numerous accomplishments, but they were not what she had anticipated. She was not flexible enough to allow for the possibility that God might have a different and better picture in mind for her.

Looking at the life of Joseph helped her look at herself in a different light. Joseph had been wrongly sold into slavery, unjustly imprisoned, and seemingly forgotten. He had maintained his integrity and had continued to do his best.

God saw the entire quilt with all its pieces. Joseph could only see part of one piece at a time. It was not until all was revealed that Joseph could say, "God meant it for good." Can you in faith say that about your life today?

Or do you not know that your body is the temple of the Holy Spirit who is in you, whom you have from God, and you are not your own?

—1 COR. 6:19

Jim had lived as if his own needs were unimportant. He was a pastor who gave himself tirelessly to his congregation and they, in return, tirelessly took advantage of him. A woman in his congregation called him one evening wanting to borrow a crib from the nursery. It was not a problem until she expectantly requested that he deliver it to her house. She was fully capable of getting it herself, but Jim, unable to say no, was soon on his way. He resented her for asking, but he would have felt guilty refusing a request.

"You are not your own" does not mean that we belong to the whims of others. It means that we are possessed by the Holy Spirit, who guides us and directs us perfectly. We must appreciate that He directs us to say no at times and to be independent. This verse is often interpreted as one that restricts our will. In essence it is just the opposite; we are no longer held captive by the public opinion but are now free to respond in the way we believe is right.

Lord, help us to find our freedom by losing it in you.

> *Be kindly affectionate to one another with brotherly*
> *love, in honor giving preference to one another.*
> —ROM. 12:10

Perfectionists have blinders on that permit them only one point of view. Nowhere is that more evident than in their marriage relationships.

Alice was absolutely convinced that she saw things the way they really were and that it was her husband, Randy, who needed a corrected outlook on life. Especially on their sex life.

For instance, to her there was no way a couple could possibly think about becoming physically romantic when they were still undecided on which house they should buy. And even worse, sex was totally out of the question until at least twenty-four hours after a fight had ended.

But Randy could focus on sex without settling the house decision. And to him a fight could still be resolved tomorrow without letting it interfere with their evening.

Men and women were made differently. "Different" does not mean "wrong," it just means different, as Spanish and French are different languages. One is not right and the other wrong; they are simply different.

God, help me acknowledge and accept my mate's differences without defining the differences as wrong.

*For the word of God is living and powerful, and
sharper than any two-edged sword, piercing even
to the division of soul and spirit, and of joints
and marrow, and is a discerner of the thoughts
and intents of the heart.*
—HEB. 4:12

Max went by the handle Road Warrior. He was a ten-year veteran at driving the eighteen-wheeler. Like many truck drivers his was a lonely life spending many long and unpredictable hours on the road. Max had been driving since he was nineteen, six months after marrying his high school sweetheart, Katy.

Road life was not what Max expected. He had miscalculated the profit he would get and how lonely it would be without Katy. He rationalized that at least he was making more than before and he could work as much as he wanted while young. Katy had also become pregnant that first year of marriage, so Max felt even more financial pressure.

As Max sat in my office ten years later trying to save his marriage, he poured out his regrets at being driven to work for the American Dream. I encouraged Max to "let go and let God" start the healing.

Father, my heart aches with the consequences of my ambition and greed.

"Do not withhold your mercy from me, O Lord;
may your love and your truth always protect me.
For troubles without number surround me; my sins
have overtaken me, and I cannot see."
—PS. 40:11–12

Several months later Max was able to be more vulnerable and admit how his workaholism had scarred him and his family.

Max was filled with shame. What had started off great had turned awfully sour in ten years. It began by "just adding one more trip onto a busy week before heading home." This led to tension and distance in his relationship with Katy and consequently more loneliness on the road.

Max said he began to frequent pornography shops to gratify himself sexually and he also met the prostitutes that frequented some of the truck stops. Eventually he began using alcohol and drugs which were also in great supply at the truck stops.

This was what finally led Max to therapy, because he had vowed never to develop a drinking problem like his parents. Max felt a great burden lift when he "got it all out" and took comfort in reading the Psalms.

Father, I claim your promise of cleansing me from my sins if I confess. Forgive the consequences of my workaholism.

I will bless the Lord who has given me counsel;
My heart also instructs me in the night seasons.
I have set the Lord always before me;
Because He is at my right hand I shall not
*   be moved.*
—PS. 16:7–8

Max was able to confess and later give God control of his variable addictions. He then became aware of his fragmented boundaries on the road and his rigid boundaries at home.

He was grateful that Katy could forgive him. Max learned that he needed to share his needs with Katy and also listen to hers even when he was tired. Max learned that he was more important to his wife than their dream home was. This knowledge allowed him to spend less time on the road.

Max learned to set firmer boundaries on the road. With the help of other truckers he learned of Christian-oriented truck stops that catered to his needs. He found a network of friends who not only held him accountable but sincerely cared about him.

Max and Katy were grateful for all that God had done for them. Eventually they returned their thanks by taking an active leadership role in ministry to other truckers and their families.

After confession we must hand future control over to God.

> *For You, LORD, have made me glad through Your*
> *work;*
> *I will triumph in the works of Your hands.*
> —PS. 92:4

Max and Katy were grateful for the testimony the Lord had given them and looked forward to any opportunity to share it. They now run a truckers' support group for those in recovery. When Max was on the road he was often asked to speak to other groups.

Max and Katy each had a talent to see through the codependency of others and reach out to the core of their hunger for love. Each time they reached out Katy and Max were drawn closer to each other.

Occasionally they did have to be on guard against the old habits that now emerged in a new way. As soon as they became a little self-centered Max would overbook speaking engagements on the road. Just like the old days, Katy would begin to distance. Fortunately God had provided them with a loving network of friends who could spot this in a minute and give them a healthy nudge in the right direction.

_____

God is faithful to our humbly letting go of control and submitting to his way. He will do great things in you.

There is a way which seems right to a man,
But its end is the way of death.

—PROV. 14:12

Have you ever heard the saying, "Don't believe anything you hear and only half of what you see"? Things are not always as they appear. Consider the mineral pyrite, for example. It is commonly known as "fool's gold." The excitement it generates has left many a goldminer looking foolish when he discovered it was not gold after all. The music of the sirens in mythology was so irresistibly beautiful that every captivated sailor perished on the rocks.

On what basis are you making important life decisions? Are you following the whim of the day, what you read in magazines or see reported on TV? Do you drive yourself to show others that you are not as inadequate as you feel? Are you trying to gain the approval of that critical parent? Do you work too much to avoid responsibilities in other areas, such as intimate relationships?

Seek the advice of the experienced. Have you ever asked an elderly person what regrets he has or what he would do differently given the chance to do it all over again? Try it—it may save you a lot of heartache.

Remember the adage: Look before you leap.

*"The LORD gave, and the LORD has taken away;
Blessed be the name of the LORD."*

—JOB 1:21

Phil was just as surprised as I was. We had sent word ahead that our original flight was delayed and we would be coming on the next available flight three days later. The ticket agent in Johannesburg had assured us it was taken care of. It wasn't. There we sat, the only two Americans in the Swazi International Airport. Everyone else had already gone except for the baggage man who spoke no English.

The terminal was fifteen miles from the nearest town. It contained one telephone and no friendly faces. We were about to begin two years as vocational missionaries in Swaziland and no one was there to pick us up, much less welcome us. Finally, after waiting over an hour for our telephone call to be placed, someone arrived and we began our African adventure.

Job was surprised, too. He had not expected to lose his family and his fortune in one day. In verse 20 he grieved the loss. But verse 21 is an acknowledgment of his perspective. He knew he was not in ultimate control, and he didn't hold final responsibility.

Surprises often teach that. What have your surprises taught you lately?

Whatever your hand finds to do, do it with
your might; for there is no work or device or
knowledge or wisdom in the grave where
you are going.
                                        —ECCL. 9:10

Why are you reading this book? We, the authors, joked during the planning stages of it that no workaholic worth his salt would have the time to read it. Better yet, he would probably read all 366 of the devotionals in one sitting and be done with it, ready to move on to other things. For whatever reason you are reading this book, we are glad that you are.

Workaholics equate their identity with work and judge their worth by how well they perform. They are perfectionists. They do not have clear boundaries to know when to say when. They are motivated by guilt and inferiority.

I chose today's verse because a workaholic will tend to look to this verse to justify her workaholism. Justification will not be found here. God did intend for us to work and to enjoy the fruits of our labors. However, he never intended for us to lose perspective on the things most important in life—our relationship with God, our families, and our health. Work and enjoy it, but never let your performance be the basis for your identity.

Lord, thank you for work; help us to do it your way.

> *Finally, all of you be of one mind, having*
> *compassion for one another; love as brothers, be*
> *tenderhearted, be courteous; not returning evil for*
> *evil or reviling for reviling, but on the contrary*
> *blessing, knowing that you were called to this,*
> *that you may inherit a blessing.*
> —1 PETER 3:8–9

It was quite a paradox. Diane and her husband, James, were both professional musicians. They were well acquainted with blending different notes in music. Yet Diane expected James to value what she valued and think like she thought.

Perfectionists tend to like one melody. No parts, no harmonies, no extraneous notes. With Diane and James, when differences occurred, she took them personally and felt a need to "even the score." And James did his own share of staying one up on her, too. They both sang harmony and lived monotone.

Yet the Scriptures indicate that harmony is essential to relationships. The verses here endorse the inevitable differences that exist between a husband and wife. But they also indicate something else: No keeping score, no more "eye for an eye." Instead, when confronted with an insult the appropriate response is to give a blessing in return. If we respond in that way, Scriptures promise that a blessing will be inherited.

What is in store for you to inherit?

*Providing honorable things, not only in the sight of
the Lord, but also in the sight of men.*
> —2 COR. 8:21

A child asked her father, "What does 'business ethics'
mean?" "Well," explained the merchant, "it's like this.
A man comes in the store and makes a purchase. He
gives me a new twenty-dollar bill which is the right
amount and starts out. I'm turning to the cash register
when I discover that it's two twenty-dollar bills stuck
together. Now comes the business ethics—should I tell
my partner?"

The legal profession has long been accused of having ethics but no morals. The attorney must work just
as hard at getting the guilty killer off scot-free as he
does the anti-abortion demonstrator.

The Christian, on the other hand, is often shown to
have morals but no ethics. A highly visible Christian
ministry stayed on the frontlines of the abortion battle.
On the homefront it was not paying its bills on time and
then only with the coercion of a lawsuit. We should
never let our missions pass by our integrity. If God
guides he will provide.

Lord, take my silver and my gold; not a mite would I withhold.

Where no oxen are, the trough is clean;
But much increase comes by the strength of an ox.
—PROV. 14:4

Jeremy was simply tired of the hassle. There had been no major problems, no intentional hurts, no devastating disappointments, but he was tiring of the daily grind to maintain the relationship with his business partner. All Jeremy wanted to do was see the sales figures go up and keep the cash flow steady. He was tired of having to give and receive apologies.

He had once considered selling out to David and going out on his own, but he could not swing it. So for the time being he dropped the idea. Besides, David was better at the loan negotiations than he was. David had more patience than he did in dealing with the staff.

Jeremy did not see it, but he was living proof of the verse in Proverbs. Agriculturally speaking, if you have an ox in your barn, there will be water to haul, feed to carry, and manure to shovel. But there will also be strength to pull the plow in the field. If there is not an ox in the barn then the stable work is easy. But the field will not be plowed.

Who is in your stable that has to be "shoveled up after"? Granted, manure stinks, but can you pull the plow all by yourself?

. . . Who may stand in His holy place?
He . . . Who has not lifted up his soul to an idol.
—PS. 24:3–4

We football fans know the immense amount of time that goes into preparation for game day by the coaches. The coach's career is based on the win/loss column and he is under constant scrutiny by the owner and fans. The pressure to perform is incredible. Coaches spend all of their time during the season thinking of football and nothing else. Many have regretted not being there as their children were growing up.

There is tragedy in the fact that men give up everything of long-term importance for a game. The pressure to win has caused them to lose perspective. And when we follow suit and demand more from them as fans, we are no better. We have lost perspective too.

One of the keys to a fulfilling life is to love the work that you do. Just be sure to keep your work in the proper perspective.

Lord, help us to keep the only perspective that will assure us of contentment—yours.

> *So He does not regard the offering anymore,*
> *Nor receive it with good will from your hands.*
> *Yet you say, "For what reason?"*
> *Because the LORD has been witness*
> *Between you and the wife of your youth,*
> *With whom you have dealt treacherously;*
> *Yet she is your companion*
> *And your wife by covenant.*
>
> —MAL. 2:13–14

Derek was president of a growing computer company. He also acted as general contractor and built his own house. He was paying for the house by doing consulting on the side.

He knew how to manage time. He had to. To do all that and still cheat on his wife several times per week necessitated the wise use of his time. The second day after Derek's marriage he had a sexual encounter.

Derek was an extreme case, but he was also typical of most workaholics. He acted like an addict in many areas of his life. In general, when a workaholic finds something he or she likes, be it sin or not, he will usually become engrossed in it.

Lord God, help me to not be deceived and help me to intentionally and continually honor my mate.

"The wolf also shall dwell with the lamb,
The leopard shall lie down with the young goat,
The calf and the young lion and the fatling together;
And a little child shall lead them."   —ISA. 11:6

One of the greatest challenges in helping codependent individuals in their recovery is to help them make amends with their children. Workaholics are some of the most difficult to treat because of their strong "reality orientation" in which only productive pursuits make sense.

In their book *Kids Who Carry Our Pain,* Drs. Hemfelt and Warren talk about permission to explore. This concept refers to giving our children permission to explore inside themselves and compare this to their outside world.

Recovering workaholics can restore their relationships with their young children by spending more unstructured time with them and by spending more time in creative play. By unstructured time we mean time where you just hang out with your kids and do what they want. They may ask you to read to them or play with their toy cars and trucks. This leads to creative play. If you are playing with trucks or action figures, follow their lead. They'll love being the teacher.

Father, teach me through my children how to be a child.

> *But you, be strong and do not let your hands be*
> *weak, for your work shall be rewarded!*
> —2 CHRON. 15:7

Every time Kevin turned around his father, Bill, was screaming at him or someone else in the family. Kevin had reached a point where he actually looked forward to his dad being away on business.

He was even more adamant now that his father was trying to make amends. Bill was frustrated and hurt that his son wouldn't give him a chance. He was in a support group and family therapy and desperately wanted Kevin to let him back into his life.

Teens and older adult children are often the most difficult to reconcile with during our recovery from our addiction. We must remember they have learned to adapt to our self-centered behavior.

It helps if we remember they must go through the same recovery that we do. They, too, are getting in touch with negative thoughts and feelings about not having their needs met. We need to confess our past mistakes and then just be available. Even just sitting with them asking a periodic question about some event in their life can put you on the right course.

Are you thinking of your children's needs, now that you're making amends?

*"Look, Lord . . . if I have taken anything from
anyone by false accusation, I restore fourfold."*
—LUKE 19:8

We counselors often hear a spouse or adult child describing a loved one with these words: "I never heard her say, 'I'm sorry.'" Perhaps you know someone who fits this description. They may apologize in their own way, of course, the most popular, perhaps, by doing or buying something. Then the offense is usually forgotten. Neither of these concessions is adequate, however, because neither addresses the issues.

The fifth step of the Twelve Step program is, "Admitted to God, to ourselves and to another human being the exact nature of our wrongs." It is essential that we confess our transgressions to the Lord. It is from him that we receive forgiveness. It is also important to confess our wrongs to others, specifically the recipients of our actions. To confess to another for accountability is also a healthy sign of repentance. The act of confessing the pain we carry lifts a tremendous burden from our hearts. We must also be exact. To say, "Forgive me if I hurt you" is too general. Say specifically how you offended and why you know it to be wrong. Your humble honesty is the doorway to peace and intimate relationships.

———————————

Lord, help me to be totally honest when apologizing to others.

> *I beseech you therefore, brethren, by the mercies of God, that you present your bodies a living sacrifice, holy, acceptable to God, which is your reasonable service.*
> —ROM. 12:1

Jerry had been a problem to his parents since his teen years and had never held a job for more than eighteen months. He was addicted to work, money, alcohol, and more. Then he was confronted and he sought help, acknowledged his powerlessness, and embraced God.

But he had never learned how to submit. Even though he wanted to submit to God now, he just did not know how to do so. His motives were right, but he did not feel able to submit.

The problem he experienced is explained in the Romans verse. Jerry thought that before he could present himself to God he had to become "holy and acceptable" to God. Anything else seemed hypocritical. It took a while for him to grasp the concept that the act of submitting was what made him holy and acceptable. Cleaning up his life would come later and would be orchestrated by God.

Do you have Jerry's problem? Do you feel you are not yet good enough to submit to God? Do not wait till you think you are because you will never come to that point.

My dishonor is continually before me,
And the shame of my face has covered me,
Because of the voice of him who reproaches and
   reviles,
Because of the enemy and the avenger.
                              —PS. 44:15–16

Patricia was the regional champ at moving plastic ware. She was an expert at selling more products and signing up more distributors than anyone in the state. She got into the business ten years before, in order to supplement her husband's income after the purchase of their first home.

At first Patricia worked from home, limiting herself to one party a week. Now her husband was threatening to leave, and her teenage children didn't even know her. All she could say was "But the money and perks were so good."

Over the years she had managed to schedule an average of eight parties per week, although twelve was her record! Patricia did these parties both afternoons and evenings, rationalizing that she was supplementing their income. First she worked to help with the mortgage, then for a few extras, and now for a cruise for her and her husband. The truth was, Patricia was addicted to plastic ware, and her husband was sick of it.

Patricia admitted she was powerless over her drive to work. Have you admitted your powerlessness?

September 24 – IS THERE A VOLUNTEER?

Therefore let him who thinks he stands take heed lest he fall.
—1 COR. 10:12

The air was tense with the silence. The scene was the weekly supervisor's meeting that included the authors of this book. The director had just asked for a volunteer to take on a small project. No one spoke up. We were all busy enough to satisfy our need for adventure, but the temptation was felt by each one to volunteer to take on the project. Finally Angela, our child psychologist, spoke up. "I can do it," she said. The fact was that as the only child psychologist on staff, she had to carry the heaviest load of us all. Later we teased her about volunteering, self-righteously proclaiming our discipline to refrain from compulsive volunteerism. We are recovering workaholics, we implied tongue-in-cheek, and we have learned to master ourselves—shouldn't you . . . ? The truth is, we would have volunteered for the project had it been a challenge, regardless of the present workload. The reason we didn't volunteer was that it was a boring project.

The same desires and temptations are still irrationally at work in us regardless of our rational understanding of their presence. Keep this verse in mind today as you face the challenges of the day.

When you recognize your weaknesses you are strongest.

*"And this is eternal life, that they may know You,
the only true God, and Jesus Christ whom You have
sent."*
—JOHN 17:3

There is a product whose reputation is almost unsurpassed by any other. You know it: Coca-Cola. And virtually everyone in the world has heard of this soft drink.

Amazing, isn't it? Hard work and commitment have paid off for the company who makes, bottles, and promotes "The Real Thing." The real thing? Is a soft drink the real thing?

Obsessive people confuse the real thing with a worthy second- or third-place finisher. Their priorities may be close to correct, but off just enough to cause problems. A commonly misplaced priority is the spiritual area of life. Other concerns cry louder for attention and since "the squeaky wheel gets the grease," the priority becomes misplaced.

But according to John 17:3, the top priority in life has to do with eternal life and knowing the only true God and the Savior he sent.

In reality, how does that compare to the "real thing," the top priority in your life?

To everything there is a season,
A time for every purpose under heaven. . . .
—ECCL. 3:1

I am an avid jogger and have been so since high school. At one time I gave serious consideration to running the Pittsburgh Marathon. I had enjoyed running in ten-kilometer races but saw this larger quest as a challenge.

I eventually decided one summer to begin training for a race scheduled for the following spring. Each week I added to my daily mileage, saving each weekend for a longer run. By year's end I was running six miles per day and ran twelve to fifteen miles on weekends. Then I was confronted with an important decision. If I wanted to accomplish my goal I would be adding seven to ten hours per week of training on top of my career responsibilities. I had failed to count the cost prior to starting my quest, and I decided to put it on hold. I did this without much regret because of my commitment to a greater priority—my family. Somehow I was satisfied knowing I could go back at some later period and try again.

How many times prior to this experience had I felt guilty or like a failure for not completing my objective!

How often does my work resemble my marathon training, where I lose sight of more important objectives? Lord, help me to be only your disciple.

*"I alone am left. . . . Yet I have reserved seven
thousand in Israel, all whose knees have not
bowed to Baal."*   —1 KINGS 19:14, 18

Elijah was in the throes of depression, a sign of burnout. A great man of faith, he soon found himself in a pit
that many of us fall into. He felt indispensable. He had
to feel pretty good on Mt. Carmel with the prophets of
Baal. He showed them a great exhibition of God's
power in the burning of the altar and proving false the
450 prophets of Baal. It must have made him feel quite
significant. The feeling of indispensability is related directly to our feeling of significance. The more indispensable we feel we are the more we perceive how
significant we are.

I think feeling indispensable gets a person off the
track more easily than anything else. The saying "You
can be replaced" is a very humbling one, but a necessary thought to keep in mind as we are doing our
work.

*Let us celebrate the fact that God chooses us to do what we are doing
and keep in mind that it is an honor above all others.*

> *Trust in the L*ORD *with all your heart,*
> *And lean not on your own understanding;*
> *In all your ways acknowledge Him,*
> *And He shall direct your paths.*
> —PROV. 3:5–6

King Solomon, described as the wisest man ever, instructed us not to lean on our own understanding. He did not tell us not to *use* our understanding, just not to lean on it. If we trust in the Lord he will straighten out our crooked lives.

Dan had been a jet-pilot instructor. He told the story of a young man who wanted to become a flying ace. He had a ways to go, because he used his instincts more than he used his instruments. One day Dan was riding in the plane with this skilled young pilot. The rookie almost slammed them straight into the ground. He had become disoriented, thought a field of wheat was the sky, and was streaking straight down. He didn't check his instruments.

Dan pulled them out, but just barely. The rookie had fought him for control even to the last instant. Our understanding is like the exceptional skill of that new pilot. It can become disoriented and without a set of instruments, trusting in God, we can pilot ourselves to disaster.

Dear God, help me to use my understanding but help me to trust in you and your Word.

> *"Come to Me, all you who labor and are heavy laden, and I will give you rest."*
> —MATT. 11:28

Workaholics frequently suffer from magical thinking. One such thought is to think we are more powerful than we are. In our desire to perform well consistently we take on burdens that become difficult to bear.

The mythical character Atlas, a man who was condemned to bear the weight of the world on his shoulders, is a helpful recovery analogy. When I saw a statue of Atlas I was impressed by his hulking strength and the awkwardness of the position. As a reminder of the futility of burden bearing I sometimes ask counselees to stand in the Atlas position. They stand in a squatting position, arms behind their head, as if holding a large weight. After only a minute or two they ask if they can stop and I say no. I want them to continue bearing that impossible burden until they realize they are faced with two choices: collapse under the weight or get rid of the weight and stand up.

Like Atlas, this is the trap of the workaholic. In their own minds they are condemned to bear the weight of the world and ultimately collapse, unless they determine to get rid of the weight and stand up.

God through Christ has an easier plan. Put your burden on him.

Who shall separate us from the love of Christ? . . .
in all these things we are more than conquerors
through Him who loved us. —ROM. 8:35, 37

Ed Koch, the former mayor of New York City, used to greet constituents by asking, "How am I doin'?" instead of the customary, "How are you doing?" Koch illustrates a primary motivation of behavior that is universal: to live up to the perceived expectations of others. What makes us different from the politician is our constituencies. The mayor is concerned about all registered voters who live in his district. Our constituency, on the other hand, may not even be alive! We may be living up to the expectations of another, such as a parent, who died a long time ago.

Such is the case of Hal, who was raised in a home where the motto was "Cleanliness is next to godliness." His mother had taught him that he should express his love to her by keeping his room clean. If he left a mess, it meant that he did not love her. Mom is long dead, but Hal is as compulsive as ever about cleanliness. He is miserable and is ready to cut the strings, fortunately. Consider with Hal the wonders of today's verse. Nothing can separate us from God's love—it is unconditional. He loves us whether our rooms are dirty or spotless!

Are you trying to live up to the expectations of others?

Examine me, O LORD, and prove me;
Try my mind and my heart.
—PS. 26:2

About a year ago I began to notice a pattern in how I was relating to my children. It did not seem to matter a great deal what they did, my reactions were fairly consistent: I was mad. Sometimes I would explode outwardly, sometimes I would keep it inside. But I was constant. I was angry.

At first I thought it was due to tiredness, but I realized I was angry even when I was rested. Then I rationalized that I was unintentionally taking responsibility for some struggles at work. I made an effort not to do that. And I was still angry at my kids.

I thought I had sufficiently done my personal inventory. I knew I was perfectionistic, I knew it was difficult for me to say no and I knew I leaned toward being a people-pleaser. But I had not seen that I was angry. Now that I know about the anger it is easier to handle.

You have probably done a personal assessment before. Perhaps it is time to do another and see what your inventory may be holding that you could not have seen before.

> *For the grace of God . . . teach[es] us that, denying*
> *. . . worldly lusts, we should live . . . righteously.*
> —TITUS 2:11–12

I can't say no," workaholics often respond. "I will lose my job, people will not think I'm special, they won't need me anymore!" Isn't it ironic that "Just Say No!" the slogan we expect our children to use against peer pressure, is something foreign to our own lifestyle. We have become slaves to our work and we model the addictive cycle for our family.

Our culture has perpetuated this theme by suggesting that work is everything if you want to be a success. Many offices are run on the basis of fear—that if you don't go along with the program you can leave. This attitude feeds codependency.

If you are to recover from your workaholism you must say no. In the long run the gains you achieve will far outweigh any losses. Learn to say yes to God, trust him, and let go of control. Give yourself permission today to say no to overwork.

Lord, recovery scares me because I may lose everything. Yet in order to follow you and be a positive legacy for my children I need your help. Forgive my fears and teach me to follow you.

And being found in appearance as a man, He humbled Himself and became obedient to the point of death, even the death of the cross. Therefore God also has highly exalted Him and given Him the name which is above every name.

—PHIL. 2:8–9

Margie complained about her problem with procrastination. She worked hard, yet she never seemed to accomplish what she needed to. It frustrated her because she couldn't figure out why. One thing became evident as we talked: she did first what she liked to do best and then drudged through the rest. Margie had not learned the secret of delayed gratification. Do the difficult, the least pleasing, first. If you eat your peas first, you have the cherry cobbler to look forward to; if you eat your dessert first you may never get around to the peas. Practice delaying gratification. It is the core of self-discipline.

Jesus knew the secret of delaying gratification. He laid aside all of his benefits for thirty-three years and suffered in order to enjoy the fruits of his labors forever. Save the best for last—it may transform your day.

Let this mind be in you, which was also in Christ Jesus.

> *Who are you to judge another's servant? To his*
> *own master he stands or falls. Indeed, he will be*
> *made to stand, for God is able to make him stand.*
> —ROM. 14:4

Steve was a producer, there was no doubt about it. His superiors were thrilled, and he soon became the example for others. His wife, Betty, helped him run the operation and they both worked very hard.

Steve and Betty had no children. They wanted them eventually, but too much had to be done for the organization. When I knew them about forty people were under their supervision. Several of the employees had children.

Steve and Betty pushed everyone to do more. Those who increased their production were rewarded. Those who lagged behind were encouraged to do better. Steve and Betty couldn't understand why the employees with children seemed to have a lower output.

They had fallen into the trap of judging and comparing. Steve and Betty eventually had children; their leadership style mellowed and softened almost immediately. Their perspective had changed. They had walked in someone else's moccasins, as the saying goes.

How about you? Are you judging someone's apples on the basis of how your oranges look? Ask around and see.

*Then Jesus was led up by the Spirit into the
wilderness to be tempted by the devil.*
—MATT. 4:1

One of the most difficult feelings in recovery is the
feeling of loneliness. We feel lonely because it sometimes seems that those we esteem most in our lives
aren't excited about our desire to change.

All the significant people in our lives are dependent
on our addiction to work. Without their support, we
often feel as if we have been left to die in the desert.

Yet there is a purpose to this empty place. Time and
time again in Scripture when God is preparing his people for change, there is wilderness. Even before Christ
started his ministry, he spent forty days and nights
alone without food in the wilderness.

Our true character comes out when we eliminate
our possessions and the people in our lives. We may
feel a lack of identity without them, but if we stay close
to God during this time he will be faithful.

If we follow Christ's example in the wilderness and
seek fellowship with God, he promises to meet us at
our place of deepest need.

Lord, fill my emptiness and create the identity you have for me.

> *And the Angel of the LORD appeared to him, and said to him, "The LORD is with you, you mighty man of valor!"*
>
> —JUDG. 6:12

The setting is both a comical and somber one. Somber, in that the children of Israel had been in bondage to the Midianites for forty years and they were totally discouraged. Comical, in that God was looking at a man who was literally in the pits—the winepress—trying to thresh wheat, a task that is supposed to be done on top of a hill. Picture Gideon, covered in the chaff that was supposed to blow away when he threw the wheat overhead.

Startled by the voice, he looked up, with discouragement and fear. How odd of God to choose the words "mighty man of valor"! Then again, God knew something Gideon didn't: He knew how the story would turn out because he had written the script. He knew that Gideon would, in fact, become that great warrior, just as he knew that Abram the childless would become Abraham, "the father of a multitude"; that Simon, the little "stone" who was unstable and impetuous, would become Peter, the "rock," one of the pillars in the early Church.

———————

Lord, help us to remember that your ways always lead us far beyond what we could ever believe for ourselves.

I will praise You, for I am fearfully and
wonderfully made;
Marvelous are Your works,
And that my soul knows very well.
—PS. 139:14

Workaholism is generally accompanied by rigidity and inflexibility. It allows only one way of looking at something, only one way of solving a problem, and only one way of thinking.

If facts verified those "only one" assumptions, the rigid way of life would have some basis. One example of "more than one way" is found in the differences in how the male and female brains work. Females have a more highly developed right side of the brain and males a more highly developed left side. Women seem to be better able to access both sides of their brain simultaneously. Men tend to use only one side of their brain at a time.

The right hemisphere of the brain is where fine motor skills, emotional understanding, listening skills and speech are centered. The left side of the brain provides visual perception, gross motor skills, activity, abstract reasoning, and logic.

Do you tend toward any of these groupings of behavior and thinking? Do you see your mate using a correspondingly different set of processes?

*Also it is not good for a soul to be without
knowledge,
And he sins who hastens with his feet.*
—PROV. 19:2

Lemmings are rodents that have an internal instinct that causes them to home in on some faraway destination. They are so driven to get to that destination that they either run off cliffs or swim out to sea and die.

I felt a little like these lemmings the first time I drove in Washington. I felt as if hundreds of cars appeared out of nowhere at high speeds. I feel the same way when my caseload climbs too high—as if I'm caught on a treadmill.

If we are to recover as workaholics we must realize that we are driven by something that robs us of our choices for a balanced lifestyle. To be freed we must give God control of our work addiction and study his Scriptures for guidance. We must also seek counsel of others who are familiar with the hope and recovery that God offers.

God, I confess something drives me in destructive ways. Please take control and put me on the path of your Son, who leads to peace and joy.

*Not that we are sufficient of ourselves to think
of anything as being from ourselves, but our
sufficiency is from God.* —2 COR. 3:5

The ancient philosophers used to wonder where humans got the idea of perfection, because they recognized that no human ever experienced it. Technically, we never should have conceptualized the perfect circle or the straight line, much less recognized our own inadequacies. And yet we have. In fact, we spend the better part of our lives either focusing on what's wrong with us or trying to compensate for our inadequacies. For example, the president of the company may walk in his front door at night and transform into an insecure, confused parent.

The key to a balanced life is neither to overcompensate for inadequacies nor to deny they exist. We must learn to accept our limitations and yet at the same time strive to improve ourselves. The ability to do so rests in our own sense of security. Many of us have been raised with the idea that to admit inadequacy is a sign of weakness, and that we are only secure when we are strong.

The mind of God is just the opposite, thankfully. Our verse for today shows that God wants us to realize he alone is sufficient to provide what we desire.

Lord, thank you for your grace, which is sufficient for all my inadequacies.

How beautiful are your feet in sandals . . .
—SONG 7:1

His countenance is like Lebanon,
Excellent as the cedars.
—SONG 5:15

Men and women differ in how we view intimacy and sexuality. Typically, our Western culture places the focus of sex on technique. However, not everyone is equally interested in technique. Columnist Ann Landers once conducted a survey entitled "Snuggles or Sex?" Over 90,000 women responded to her questionnaire, and of that number more than 64,000 indicated that they thought a warm hug or a gentle touch were more important than intercourse!

The Scripture addresses this whole question of physical intimacy. In the passage where the husband Solomon describes his bride, he rarely mentions her head and face. But in the passage where the bride describes her husband, she mentions his head and face predominantly. His focus is decidedly physical and he is stimulated by sight and touch. Her focus is on his face and character. She is far more concerned about his reputation and integrity.

How do you approach your mate? Do you acknowledge your differences?

"For the heart of this people has grown dull.
Their ears are hard of hearing,
And their eyes they have closed,
Lest they should see with their eyes and hear with
*   their ears,*
Lest they should understand with their heart and
*   turn,*
So that I should heal them."   —ACTS 28:27

Numbness, the state of having no feeling, interferes with our functioning. For many of us, work deadens some pain and gives us a chance to focus on a task to pretend the pain isn't there. As workaholics we run the risk of emotionally self-destructing. Work becomes our anesthesia and we become useless in other parts of our lives.

This is what we call the addictive cycle, which begins when we use our addictive agent to numb our pains. These pains include feeling unlovable, or believing that our needs don't matter.

If we keep working excessively we can never meet our deepest emotional needs for love. God is prepared to meet our needs when we ask.

Ask God to allow you the privilege of feeling again to restore your vitality.

> *He also brought me up out of a horrible pit,*
> *Out of the miry clay,*
> *And set my feet upon a rock,*
> *And established my steps.*
>
> —PS. 40:2

Carolyn received the news that her friend Nancy had died. Nancy used to be infamous in her small Virginia hometown, a train stop built around the coal industry. She was the town prostitute who lived near the train yard. When Nancy came to Christ she never looked back. She became active in a church and it was well known that this verse was her favorite. There is also a hymn with these words and she loved to sing it. She was truly a trophy of God's grace.

Carolyn had been working through a daily Bible memorization program and as she opened her book that day to her verse to memorize, she was startled. It was none other than "Nancy's verse."

What a tribute not only to her but to the God who delights in showing his strength through those who are weak! In his timeless omniscience he brought this verse to this day, to this person to proclaim his love. What an epitaph! Have you wondered what legacy you will leave to those who care for you?

Lord, help us to remember that you still perform miracles.

If we say that we have no sin, we deceive ourselves,
and the truth is not in us.   1 JOHN 1:8

Charlie had been raised in a dysfunctional family. His dad had placed unrealistic demands on his children's performance, attitudes, and submission to him as head of his household. And from earliest memories, Charlie had been his father's scapegoat.

So Charlie married a sensitive, genuine young woman who loved him deeply. It was a good thing. Most women would not have stayed beyond the first year. As much as he had vowed never to treat others like his dad had treated him, Charlie treated his wife just as badly and often worse.

His emotional and passive abuse were deadly. He constantly berated her for being five pounds overweight. He told her that she was simply not as exciting as he thought his wife ought to be.

His wife, friends, and sometimes strangers had tried to point out what he was doing. He was convinced they were all wrong. He was a committed husband; she was the one who needed the help. He almost lost her because he would not listen to anyone.

Has more than one person been trying to talk to you about the same topic? If so, perhaps they see something you need to see.

> *If we confess our sins, He is faithful and just to*
> *forgive us our sins.*   —1 JOHN 1:9a

Charlie finally began to believe what everyone else was saying. When he saw it, his guilt level began to soar. His remorse grew, and his behavior gradually changed.

But he had done wrong; he was guilty and he knew it. And it was beginning to eat away at him. Then he and I began to talk about confession. His assumption was that confession meant to say you were sorry and not ever to do "it" again. And if you did do it again, then you had not really confessed.

It was the popular understanding about confession, but that's not what the Bible talks about in today's verse. Literally, confession means "to say the same thing." Charlie needed to say to God the same thing God thought about his sins and failures.

Charlie discovered that God essentially says two things about sin. One, he says that the act is wrong and harmful to God and to other people. Two, he says that for the one who has trusted in Jesus, his sins were forgiven because of what Christ did on the cross.

Do you need to follow those two guidelines and "say the same thing" about any sin or shortcoming in your life?

If we confess our sins, He is faithful and just to forgive us our sins and to cleanse us from all unrighteousness.

1 JOHN 1:9

Once Charlie grasped the significance and simplicity of confession, he changed dramatically in attitude and action. He still had moments when he reverted to his old patterns, but he was growing.

He learned more about sin, too. He studied and discovered the original definition of the word. It was an archery term and meant "to fall short of the target." Sin to God was when Charlie fell short of what God had in mind.

The more he used today's verse, the more he became aware of something else, too. In this short verse are actually statements about two different kinds of sin. First is the intentional, known kind of sin. He was to confess that and then would experience the forgiveness that was his because of the cross. But the second was the "all unrighteousness" phrase. That meant that as Charlie dealt with the sin he knew about, God added a fringe benefit. He cleansed and purified from the sins Charlie did not know about.

God, how completely you forgive us when we fall short of your standards. And thank you for your forgiveness of the sins we are not even aware of.

And do not be drunk with wine, in which is
dissipation; but be filled with the Spirit.
—EPH. 5:18

When Charlie used 1 John 1:9 to experience forgiveness from his sins he was exhaling; that is the process of getting rid of the stale, foul air. But if exhaling exists then a corresponding inhaling must happen.

Charlie looked at this verse today as breathing in fresh air. When Charlie became aware of a sin or shortcoming, he would first exhale. He would say the same thing about it God said: that it was wrong and that it was forgiven because of Charlie's trust in Christ's death.

Inhaling was expressed something like, "Lord, I again admit that I need you. Please fill me with your Spirit to help me avoid sinning against you." The word *filled* in the verse carries the idea of "control and empower." It is not a receiving of the Spirit of God.

Charlie and I also drew a correlation. Since we breathe physically more than once a day, we probably need to breathe spiritually more than once a day. In fact, the more spiritual work we are doing, the more frequently we should take a spiritual breath.

How about you? Would you pray Charlie's inhale prayer now?

Return to your rest, O my soul,
For the LORD has dealt bountifully with you.
—PS. 116:7

I once had a friend who was an engineer at a research facility. When he took me on a tour of the grounds I couldn't believe my eyes. There were lots of trees, green grass, botanical gardens and a spectacular view of the river. It looked like a giant playground to me. I wondered how my friend got any work done.

It wasn't until many years later that I understood that employer's wisdom. In order to be successful at research creativity is important. When employees were nurtured in an aesthetically relaxing environment, they were better stimulated to develop new ideas.

In contrast to this, we workaholics are slaves to our desks. All of life becomes production oriented. Play becomes a thing of the past and is viewed as the enemy of production. People who do manage to squeeze in some play realize that even that has been contaminated by productivity because they strive to be the best at performing even leisure activities.

Evaluate your leisure time. Is it characterized by an overemphasis on getting it over with or doing it right? Ask God to help free you in your leisure time so you may have fun again.

*Let us therefore come boldy to the throne of grace,
that we may obtain mercy and find grace to help in
time of need.*
—HEB. 4:16

Simeon Stylites was one of the early monks who set
the stage for the movement known as asceticism, the
practice of religion that is more rigid than normal.
They were the spiritual elite, who endured self-
inflicted suffering to find favor with God. Simeon was
famous for—are you ready?—living his last thirty years
on top of a pillar! Suffice it to say, the movement was
sincere—but wrong.

Step Eleven of the Twelve Step program says,
"Sought through prayer and meditation to improve our
conscious contact with God as we understood him,
praying only for knowledge of his will for us and the
power to carry that out." It is important for a person in
recovery to grasp this concept. It is the step that can
lead to the greatest personal bondage if misunderstood. Sometimes approaching God as "we understood
him" is not sufficient enough. We must approach God
on his terms whether we understand him or not. He
tells us in this verse to approach him boldly, not fearfully; he is sitting on his throne of *grace*, not judgment.
He wants to give mercy and grace when we need it
most.

Thank you, Lord, for understanding us; help us to understand you.

There is no fear in love; but perfect love casts out fear.
—1 JOHN 4:18

The more addicted to work we are, the more we fear. We fear failure at work, rejection by loved ones, illness and death, and ultimately God. We think we can control all these fears. We are masters of rationalization.

Today's text identifies the source of our problem: we have not experienced enough unconditional love. As children we learned that performance was the only way to be loved by others or, worse, to avoid punishment.

A fantasy helps me to laugh at the absurdity of trying to be in control. I take all the fears I have and paint them on the side of an imaginary locomotive going at full speed, then I imagine myself running down the track trying to get out of its way. When I reach the point of total exhaustion, I see Christ standing in a grassy field reaching out his hand to me. He asks, "Why don't you come over to the side with me? Get off that track and let's talk about it." It's such a relief to know he loves me with no strings attached and that I can let all those fears roar down the track while I rest with him in that grassy field.

Don't be afraid to share your fears with God. He will meet you by the side of the track and take away your fears.

Dear Lord, take each of my fears one by one and give me what you have for me.

> Remember now your Creator in the days of your
>   youth,
> Before the difficult days come,
> And the years draw near when you say,
> "I have no pleasure in them."   —ECCL. 12:1

Erik Erickson, the psychologist, said that should we live to die old we will die in a state of either integrity or despair. What determines our outcome is not the circumstances of life but our response to them. The earlier we determine our course of behavior and stick to it the greater our chance of ending our days in a state of integrity.

Someone once said, "The good things in life have to be paid for in advance, while the evil things are paid for—generally on the installment plan." Think about that for a moment. For us to reap the benefits of our labor we must first pay the price of hard work. To see our lives end in peace and integrity we must invest ourselves in a life of discipline and integrity. We must do what is right early on. The good things—the satisfaction of seeing our children grow psychologically and spiritually healthy, our own sense of integrity, contentment, and joy—must be paid for on the layaway plan.

Lord, show me the right responses to make in my life.

> *"Be angry, and do not sin": do not let the sun go*
> *down on your wrath.*
> —EPH. 4:26

Anger plays a large part in our work addiction. Often on the job we are models of success but on a personal level it's very different.

When we are consumed by work we become like a pressure cooker internally. When we don't get rest the pressure continues to build and we lash out at those we love. Initially we become irritated at the requests our spouses, children, or friends may make. At its extreme the anger turns into rage and we become verbally or physically abusive.

Most of us workaholics had parents who made us be compliant without acknowledging our exasperation when expectations were too high. Fearful of expressing these feelings, we converted our energy into ultra-compliant behavior. Internally, we seethed with anger, victims of a vicious cycle with no hope of having our dependency needs met.

Take stock of those areas of your life where you get angry. Then ask God to show you the roots of this anger.

*Do not fear, little flock, for it is your Father's good
pleasure to give you the kingdom.*
—LUKE 12:32

The British have a custom called the "command performance." At the queen's whim, an actor or artist may
be called upon to render his service to the throne regardless of his prior commitments. In the old days, to
refuse to do so could result in dire consequences. Likewise, if the court jester ceased to be amusing he was
out of a job. When he performed he performed to
please the king and gave little regard to his own personal needs. Think of the pressure that must have been
on those performers!

A common characteristic for the workaholic is the
motivation to perform as if his life hinged on what
others think. Diane, an articulate, intelligent accoun-
tant, said her job was killing her but would not think of
leaving because she was afraid she would look like a
failure to others. In reckless abandon to her own wel-
fare, she threw herself into her work. Her only motivation was to please her perceived royalty: her
indifferent and workaholic management. Like the
jester she could only look forward to being cast aside
when they grew tired of her.

*God does not command us to please him for acceptance. He has al-
ready accepted us for his pleasure.*

*"You shall not bow down to them nor serve them.
For I, the LORD your God, am a jealous God,
visiting the iniquity of the fathers on the children to
the third and fourth generations of those who hate
Me."*
—EX. 20:5

Today's society demands that children cope, succeed, achieve, and win. The price children must pay is dangerous.

The children of the eighties and nineties are forced to deal with more and to do it better, faster, and earlier than their parents' generation. Today's children must learn how to live with sex, single-parent homes, blended families, and failure many years earlier than their parents. And their parents did not even have to deal with some of what is the norm for today.

Traditions have broken down. Long-standing mores have changed radically overnight, and the children are paying the price.

I believe that is what God was warning when he inspired the verse for today. It comes at the very beginning of the Ten Commandments. It is actually stated in the context of the consequences of idolatry. *Addiction* is just a watered-down term for idolatry. Workaholism and perfectionism are addictions/idolatries.

Lord, help us to stop running up an expensive bill for our children to pay.

> *Thus also faith by itself, if it does not have works,*
> *is dead.*
> —JAMES 2:17

For Christians with a work addiction this verse is a curse if taken out of context. Work addicts use this verse to rationalize working harder and often fear that if they don't work hard enough it will prove they have no faith and God will not accept them. This could not be further from the truth! If you read all of chapter 2 in James you will see that the emphasis is on showing mercy. Because we are saved by grace we work for others out of a knowledge of being loved by God first.

Our work accomplishment means nothing unless we are motivated by a sense of being loved. Loving others then has no strings attached.

At the office I do my work to the best of my ability without concern for the outcome. This lets me be free to leave on time and enjoy my time with family and others.

Lord, as I receive more of your unconditional love I realize how merciful you are to me and how unconditional your love is. Help me to remember that what you accomplished on the cross for me should be my motivation.

That you may approve the things that are excellent, that you may be sincere and without offense till the day of Christ.
—PHIL. 1:10

I have a gag program in my computer that gives me a Murphy's Law every time the machine boots. My favorite one says, "Sincerity is the key to success: the more sincere you are the more people you can fool." We laugh at this because we all relate to it to some degree. It does seem to be the underlying strategy in advertising, politics, and even religion. The word *sincere* is from the Latin *sine cera* meaning "without wax." It originated in the days of the marketplace where white porcelain was sold. Inferior pieces had hairline cracks that were filled with a pearly white wax by the crafty merchants. When the object was held to the light, the arteries of wax were revealed. The good stuff was "without wax"—sincere.

The stress of overwork can cause principled believers to lose the integrity they once valued. If we are not careful we may find ourselves doing the things that are deplored by God. There are few things as painful as hearing word spread about us that "the Christian is the last person to trust."

Lord, deliver us from the temptations of greed and quick success. Thank you for the grace and commitment to help us succeed in "the things that are excellent."

> *Be of the same mind toward one another. Do not*
> *set your mind on high things, but associate with the*
> *humble.*
>   —ROM. 12:16

Wilson was a gifted administrator, speaker, and visionary. He was also easily threatened. He functioned well as long as no one questioned him too much, and as long as others responded to him according to his expectations. That style of leadership had served him well while he was in the military, but people do not follow authority like soldiers.

Wilson had asked a subordinate to tell him his opinion of Wilson's visionary and speaking responsibilities. And the subordinate had totally misunderstood. The subordinate had thought Wilson meant what he had asked. But he did not.

Wilson never wanted to hear of any flaws others detected in him. His fearfulness and low self-esteem would never allow that. Wilson only wanted to hear how well he was doing. But the subordinate was honest, and it cost him his position. Wilson could not stand the perceived loss of face to an employee.

Are you easily threatened by honest feedback? Do you shut the mouths of those who say what you do not want to hear?

Do not be wise in your own eyes;
Fear the LORD and depart from evil.
—PROV. 3:7

Wilson was acting out what Dr. David Elkind calls in the book *The Hurried Child* his very own "personal fable," which is the result of living in front of an "imaginary audience." These two distinctly different mental operations commonly occur in self-centered, performance-oriented people.

The "imaginary audience" operation takes place when a person confuses what he is thinking with what everyone else is thinking. The self-centered person thinks everyone is just as concerned about him as he is. It is a way of bolstering a faltering ego when no one else will do it.

The result of this is the emergence of the "personal fable." A self-conscious person believes that if everyone is always concerned with what he does, he must indeed be a very special person with outstanding ability. And since that ability is so highly developed, no one could possibly disagree with the person and be correct.

The Scriptures warn us that we are really not such hot stuff. They tell us we have deceived ourselves. Do you perform in front of an imaginary audience? Do you live out a personal fable?

> *The humble He guides in justice,*
> *And the humble He teaches His way.*
> —PS. 25:9

Nothing can be more frustrating than realizing at the last minute that you have a schedule change. You thought you had gotten the time right for an event, but when you check you discover that you blew it. At first you're angry and frustrated as you try to sort through how this could happen. The perfectionistic part of you wants to find someone to blame, but there isn't time for that now. You have to decide which event to attend. No matter what you decide someone is going to be disappointed or upset.

These kinds of decisions seem to come into our lives more than we want, and they always serve as reminders of our humble humanity. You have to be honest with yourself and others in a hospitable way. Then once you make a decision you must go through the humbling experience of admitting your incompetence. You have to try to reconcile the conflict to others as soon as time permits. You now realize more than before that loss is a necessary part of life and must be experienced and not denied.

Father, please guide me through these difficult decisions of daily life when I or others fail to communicate.

*And I took the little book out of the angel's hand
and ate it, and it was as sweet as honey in my
mouth. But when I had eaten it, my stomach
became bitter.*
                                        —REV. 10:10

Things are seldom as they appear. Mythology is filled
with examples of illusions. The frog is a prince; the
beautiful woman is a witch in disguise. You are made
an offer that is too good to be true. "It will only take a
minute." "I'll pay you back Friday."

A certain restlessness in every person causes us
never to be satisfied with our lot. In many ways this is
good; it is the impetus for what we call progress. There
is also a gullibility that goes along with it that causes us
to believe that "it's just got to work." Jackie Gleason
personified this mindset as Ralph Kramden on "The
Honeymooners," who always schemed to get rich
quick but always got burned. Unfortunately, many a
person has sacrificed life and limb to achieve high status only to be grossly disappointed with the fruits in
the end.

The verse for today indicates that what may be
sweet to the taste may ultimately end in heartburn.
Check out the validity of your goals before you set
them. Is it worth the price you may have to pay?

Lord, give us the wisdom to see things from your point of view.

> *"Peace I leave with you, My peace I give to you. . . .*
> *Let not your heart be troubled."*
> —JOHN 14:27

Work addiction is not limited to those who work outside the home. Homemakers can become workaholics too.

Do you have an obsession with cleanliness that others don't seem to appreciate? Are you always thinking ahead to the next chore from dawn to dusk? If this is the case you may be making your family miserable. They probably see you as a cleaning machine that can't relax, and they may also learn to become codependent on your cleaning efficiency. Finally, your own needs go unchecked and you rarely get the appreciation you feel you deserve.

I have found it helpful when feeling overwhelmed with household duties to sit down with other family members, negotiate standards of cleanliness, and delegate responsibilities. Children need to be taught new skills that are age-appropriate. When the job is done it is also important to reward everyone with an activity that is fun or relaxing.

Lord, help me see the harm I do to myself and those around me by constantly cleaning. Help me learn to relate to others and depend on their help.

And He gave them their request,
But sent leanness into their soul.
—PS. 106:15

I noticed a number of late-model cars for sale sitting out in front of my bank. Most of them were the sporty type—Camaros, Mustangs, and the like—and had been repossessed because the owners couldn't keep up with the payments. At the time of purchase the monthly payment probably seemed small in comparison to the allure of the shiny new car on the showroom floor. But as time passed the attraction wore off and the payment began to bear down on the owner until she finally had to release the car.

How easy it is to fall into the trap of strong desire! Our judgment becomes clouded and we find ourselves caught in situations that quickly enslave us. The Israelites began to take the provision of God for granted. He had been providing them with manna, a miracle food the Lord sent from heaven daily. The people tired of it and demanded meat. They were so relentless about it that he gave it to them, but there was a price to pay. They felt less fulfilled by the meat than the manna.

How about you? Are you asking for something that might eventually be a burden on you?

You had better be careful what you ask for—you might get it.

> *"I am the vine, you are the branches. He who abides in Me, and I in him, bears much fruit; for without Me you can do nothing."*
>
> —JOHN 15:5

Webster defines the word *nothing* as "something that does not exist; an object, person, event, or remark of no or slight value." I heard another description of it: "a zero with the rim kicked off."

It was Jesus who said that apart from him we could do nothing. What did he mean? After all, I know of plenty of God-snubbing people who have made a great deal of money, discovered mysteries of the universe, and done great things for humankind. What could he mean by saying we could do nothing apart from him?

Part of Webster's definition solves this. "An object, person, event, or remark of *no or slight value.*" Jesus is putting accomplishments and productivity, important as they are, in perspective. He is saying that the only things of lasting value have some link to him; that there must be a spiritual aspect to our lives.

Most atheists and agnostics have no spiritual resources at their disposal. But many churchgoing people in America today have no true, personal, spiritual reservoir either. How about you? What is your spiritual condition?

Teach me Your way, O LORD;
I will walk in Your truth;
Unite my heart to fear Your name.
—PS. 86:11

Last year my wife, two sons, and I took up golf. At our first lesson our instructor told us to show him how we would hit the ball. I focused carefully on holding the club, hitting the ball, and reaching the target. Then I swung, and the ball went two feet!

My instructor immediately said that I would have a difficult time because golf was illogical. This was true, for each time I applied my logic to how each new drill would affect the flight of the ball I was wrong.

The same is true in our recovery from a work addiction. Many of the suggestions made for recovery seem illogical and awkward at first. We are frustrated when we don't get the desired results the first time. When we are so programmed to look for outcome we miss the smaller steps of progress along the way and the pure enjoyment of learning a new thing.

God has already taken care of the final outcome for your life through Christ. All you have to do is to obey his teaching for today and he will see that the outcome is reached.

> *All things are lawful for me, but all things are not*
> *helpful. All things are lawful for me, but I will not*
> *be brought under the power of any.*
> —1 COR. 6:12

Have you said no to anyone recently?" I asked Brenda, who was overwhelmed with responsibility. She hemmed and hawed and shifted in her seat.

"I feel one coming on now," I said, anticipating her response. We both laughed. It was not a laughing matter, however. Brenda had difficulty refusing a request. In fact, she said that the words she hates to hear most are "Could you just. . . ." She hears those words from her boss all the time.

Brenda is not alone. For some, to say no is like rejecting the person. Others need to be in on the action, whatever it is. Others don't refuse a request because they are afraid they may never be asked to participate again.

The apostle Paul prioritized what was important, set his focus on it, and stayed the course. We too have the freedom to choose what we want to do; we also have the freedom *not* to choose. Try saying the "N" word a few times.

———————————

Lord, give us the wisdom to recognize the important things and the strength to resist the rest.

O foolish Galatians! Who has bewitched you that you should not obey the truth, before whose eyes Jesus Christ was clearly portrayed among you as crucified?

—GAL. 3:1

Jerry had been had. He had grown up in the forest and had never in his life seen a tree. Jerry was a successful traveling preacher who was gifted in speaking and able to sway crowds. He did so with integrity. He did not use either his position or his gifts to unethically raise money. He was honest in his relationship with his wife and never was unfaithful to her. But he had never seen a tree.

He had grown up in a good, Christian family. He had met Jesus the Savior at an early age and had a genuine zeal to tell the world about him. But Jerry operated under two assumptions: first, that his faith in Jesus Christ would allow him admittance into heaven. So far, so good. But his second assumption was that God was only pleased with Jerry because of the things he did for God.

The book of Galatians was written for people like Jerry. The "tree" he had never seen before counseling was this fact: God differentiated between *what* Jerry did and *who* Jerry was. Jerry came to understand God was satisfied with him because they had a relationship.

Jerry had been had because he was trying to earn God's ongoing satisfaction. Have you been had?

> *My soul, wait silently for God alone,*
> *For my expectation is from Him.*
> —PS. 62:5

Work addicts often consider it a virtue to skip the lunch hour. This is just one of many denials of basic dependency needs. To think that we are super-human and can run all day on adrenaline is fantasy. Yet many times lunch hour is used to finish that report or make one more phone call.

Part of our recovery is learning to appreciate break times and realizing our job future doesn't depend on us completing one more task over lunch hour.

You must reclaim this small portion of time in mid-day and nurture yourself. A little food, a walk, or some fellowship with friends will help. If other Christians are accessible to your workplace a lunchtime devotional can be very refreshing. Others may enjoy calling family or friends or finding a quiet place to close their eyes and take a snooze.

Above all, when you structure this into your schedule you must avoid talking about work. Instead, talk about family news or other activities outside work.

Lord, you were a model of balance between work and rest. You spent time alone and time in fellowship with those closest to you. Guide me to take time to be fed in the middle of my day.

*Therefore do not cast away your confidence, which
has great reward. For you have need of endurance,
so that after you have done the will of God, you
may receive the promise.*   —HEB. 10:35–36

Another problem associated with lunch hour is the
addictive or codependent office. At healthy organizations break times are encouraged. However, other organizations function much like the family of addicts. In
these organizations work can be an addictive behavior
for large groups of people. This results in incredible
peer pressure to work hard. Employees get the message that if they want to advance or be successful
they'd better keep working.

Pay attention to the kinds of organizational behaviors that draw you back into your addictive cycle. You
may need to address this with your peers and superiors. If the organization doesn't support this you may
need to make some serious choices about your future
at that place of work.

To weather this storm you may want to establish
support groups with others in your office to help you
resist the temptation to return to your addiction.

*Father, please open my eyes to the environment where I work. Help
me be aware of ways it may encourage me not to resi*

> *Examine yourselves as to whether you are in
> the faith. Prove yourselves. Do you not know
> yourselves, that Jesus Christ is in you?—unless
> indeed you are disqualified.*   —2 COR. 13:5

There seem to be two types of dysfunctional people. Some people say that the responsibility to solve the problem lies elsewhere; others say the problem is all theirs. Some take too much responsibility for problems, others not enough. The not-so-odd fact is that they tend to attract each other and marry.

Life is full of problems and every person has more than enough to deal with. The basis of success and happiness in life is willingness to acknowledge our problems and resolutely take responsibility *for our part*. We can only do this accurately after regular self-examination. This is the key to determining accurate boundaries.

What group are you in? We all have a bit of both in us, naturally. Do you have the courage to stop long enough to examine yourself? It may be the key to happiness.

_____

*Lord, help us to take responsibility for what we should; give us the
wisdom to know when.*

> *"Woe to you. . . . For you pay tithe of mint and anise and cummin, and have neglected the weightier matters of the law: justice and mercy and faith."*
> —MATT. 23:23

Shortly after college graduation I moved to Swaziland, Africa, as a missionary. I had a wreck in Africa, and I have come to realize that the reason for my accident is the same reason that perfectionism, workaholism, and obsessions cause such havoc in so many lives.

The accident was my fault. The problem? I was driving according to rules that did not apply to where I was living. You see, in Swaziland it is correct to drive on the lefthand side of the road. When you make a righthand turn there, you cross the oncoming lane of traffic. Having driven in America, I was used to watching out only for pedestrians when making a righthand turn.

But this day I saw no pedestrians in the way and made a right turn directly into the path of an oncoming vehicle that I was not even looking for. Fortunately, no one was seriously injured.

Perfectionism and its two counterparts are like that. Rules that do not apply are followed and accidents result.

Are you following marketplace guidelines and neglecting justice and mercy in your relationships?

*Therefore I run thus: not with uncertainty. Thus I
fight: not as one who beats the air.*

—1 COR. 9:26

Racquetball has been around for years but I only discovered it two years ago. It's a combination of tennis and pinball and is played in a white room with high ceilings and hardwood floors.

The racquetball court has proven to be an excellent classroom for me. I have learned many lessons about how to approach life there. For example, I have learned that the game can be played intensely but it can also be enjoyed. You can do your best to beat your opponent and still compliment him on his good plays. If you are too lazy you will miss some opportunities to score. If you try too hard you will get in your own way and make unnecessary mistakes. It is patience and not power that produces the control necessary to improve as a player. Some days you can do no wrong; other days you feel it would have been better not to show up at all.

The apostle Paul is using sports as an example of life too. He is comparing the Olympic events of ancient Greece with life. There is much to be gained from participation in sports; exercise, stress reduction, and coping skills to carry back into life. Enjoy a sport—but do not work at it!

We tend to play at our work and work at our play.

He who covers his sins will not prosper,
But whoever confesses and forsakes them
will have mercy. —PROV. 28:13

Ryan had always dreamed of being a Top Gun, but that was twenty-five years ago. Now he was looking at divorce papers from Judy. He hoped he could change her mind, but he was pessimistic. After all, since his retirement from the Navy he rarely saw his family. He was frequently on the road and during those long lonely hours he had been involved in three extramarital relationships.

Judy had been through this before early in their marriage as Ryan struggled to be a Top Gun pilot. "Hard work and fast women" was his motto. Until now he never thought about where this came from. He remembered that his father had been a crack pilot and always encouraged him to be a Top Gun. That dream always made him feel special to his father. He also felt special when his father told him secrets. Frequently Ryan's father told him not to tell his mother he stopped to "have a few with the boys."

Now Ryan realized how guilty he felt when he saw his mother in pain after arguing with his father about his whereabouts. He now realized he too was keeping secrets from those he loved and it was time to confess.

Father, I claim the promises you offer for genuine confession.

> *Do not lie to one another, since you have put off*
> *the old man with his deeds, and have put on the*
> *new man who is renewed in knowledge according*
> *to the image of Him who created him.*
> —COL. 3:9–10

Ryan's support group encouraged him to level with Judy in spite of the divorce papers. This ex-fighter jockey had always been trained to keep his emotions out of the cockpit. Ryan still functioned like he was in the cockpit and couldn't afford to get emotionally involved.

Now he felt vulnerable—like flying without instruments. He knew the group was right so he shared with Judy what he had learned. Ryan told her about the secrets he had kept for his father. He said he realized by lying to her he was hurting her the same way his mother had been hurt. He went on to share how inadequate he felt when he had failed to be a Top Gun. He realized he used his work and sex to hide these negative emotions.

Judy forgave him but, due to her own pain, she insisted they start joint counseling. Ryan was elated and gave her a big hug. He knew they had a tough road ahead but was thankful.

When we confess our past wrongs we must do so completely at the mercy of the other person. We must also expect to change our actions.

But as for me, I will walk in my integrity;
Redeem me and be merciful to me.
—PS. 26:11

Judy was angry and she had been angry for a long time. Emotionally Ryan could feel himself withdrawing. When I noticed this, I asked him to share what he was thinking. Ryan struggled but eventually shared that he felt inadequate when Judy was angry.

Ryan also discovered that when he felt inadequate on a business trip he wanted to talk to Judy but felt guilty because she was angry at him for not being there. This made him feel more inadequate which then led him to have fantasies if he saw another woman.

Each spouse had to look at the part he or she played in the breaking down of communication. In Ryan's case, he had to be honest with Judy about his feelings of inadequacy at home or on the road. As this unfolded they learned to trust each other again.

Lord, vulnerability scares me, because I like to project an image of perfection. Teach me to be honest.

> *My brethren, take the prophets, who spoke in the*
> *name of the Lord, as an example of suffering and*
> *patience.*
> —JAMES 5:10

A popular bumper sticker said, "life's a [blankety—blank] and then you die." It articulated (rather crudely) what we all feel, and it's true. Life is full of problems. How we respond to this thought will make all the difference in our ability to negotiate life's problems. Our natural response is to deny the pain of life and avoid facing up to it. We have an inherent drive to find pleasure and avoid pain. We must learn not to give in to it. Discipline is required to face problems in life and not run from them. The tendency to avoid problems and pain is the basis of all addictions, including overwork.

Scripture admonishes us to look back on how others dealt with the problem of pain and suffering. The prophets knew that there was a better place prepared for them and that this problem-paved life was the road to it. The hope gave them the courage and patience to discipline themselves to face and endure the pain on the way. Let's follow their example, shall we?

Carl Jung once said, "Neurosis is always a substitute for legitimate suffering."

Ont

~~Craddock~~ Craddock, Fred, F[...]
Overhearing the Gospel

A false balance is an abomination to the LORD,
But a just weight is His delight.
—PROV. 11:1

Steve loved the game of croquet and was skilled and practiced at it. He even had a court in his backyard. He would play anyone, anytime, and he would always play with the same level of intensity. When you played Steve the croquet was rarely relaxing.

Steve did everything like he played croquet: all-out. Anything he did was done well and thoroughly and his superiors never had to double-check his work. He knew how to laugh, was creative, and, as you might expect, was a self-starter full of initiative.

But he constantly worked at taking care of his own temple—his own body. His wife used to remind him that he needed to balance the scales: work hard and then play some. He had his own way of relaxing, he would say. And he did, and it worked for him.

You may be as intense as Steve. Have you found a way of relaxing that works for you? How do you balance taking care of yourself with taking care of your responsibilities? And which takes priority?

> *There is nothing better for a man than that he*
> *should eat and drink, and that his soul should*
> *enjoy good in his labor. This also, I saw, was*
> *from the hand of God.*
> —ECCL. 2:24

Danny related his father's disapproval of his buying a new car. Danny budgeted his money, saved it, and gave to the Lord. He worked hard and one of his few pleasures in life was his car. He enjoyed driving it and he loved to polish it. To him it was money well spent, but to his father it was unnecessary. His dad felt that money should be saved and kept for a rainy day. "Trouble is always on the horizon," he said, "and you never know when you will need it." Dan wanted his dad to enjoy the car with him, but all he got was an aloof disapproval that made him feel guilty.

Scripture does not support such fearful living exhibited by Dan's father. While common sense does dictate saving, it does not dictate paranoia. Solomon, who researched the meaning of life by attempting to live it to the hilt, concluded his findings with this verse. Likewise, we need to learn to relax and not feel guilty for it.

―――――――――――

God, give me the freedom to choose the method for relaxing that suits me best.

> *Put off, concerning your former conduct, the old man which grows corrupt according to the deceitful lusts.*
>
> —EPH. 4:22

Leslie had a difficult time letting go. Her addictive personality did not want to remove the distortions she had developed in her desire to experience love, security, and acceptance. She temporarily met them through her compulsiveness and she was not yet choosing to have those needs met in any other way.

But the more she worked at meeting legitimate needs through illegitimate means, the less satisfaction she experienced and the more frustration she felt. Finally, because all else had not given her enough, she began to consider that God was able to meet her needs.

Leslie's breakthrough came when she audibly asked God to remove these addictions from her life so that she could worship him instead.

How about you? Step Six is only the willingness to exchange false gods for the real God. Are you willing yet?

> *Therefore humble yourselves under the mighty*
> *hand of God, that He may exalt you in due time,*
> *casting all your care upon Him, for He cares for*
> *you.*   1 PETER 5:6–7

The way Leslie asked God to remove the old, established defects made all the difference. She had hesitated earlier because she thought she would have to humiliate herself in front of God, her husband, and possibly her family and friends. When she learned that humiliation and humility are distinctly different, the relief itself was an experience of freedom to her.

By this time it was almost easy for her. Since she had tried for so long and in so many ways to have her inner needs met and had not succeeded, she already knew her helplessness. All she added to her own sense of inability was an acknowledgment of God's ability and concern for her.

Leslie's husband noticed it first. Her anger subsided gradually and her patience increased. She had actually been improving for almost a month before she could see it.

Have you asked God to clean out your flaws? How have you asked him? Humility and helplessness are the package we are to bring to him.

> *"When I passed by you again and looked upon you, indeed your time was the time of love. . . . I swore an oath to you and entered into a covenant with you, and you became Mine," says the Lord* GOD.
> —EZEK. 16:8

Bob reflected over the past week. For five days he left the house before his five-year-old daughter was awake and returned after she was asleep. He was approaching a deadline for a project, but then he always was. He loved his little Amy and would do nothing purposely to hurt her. He worked so hard, in fact, because he knew the costs of sending a child to college today, and the money required to keep his family clothed and fed was incredible. Besides, he felt that his wife was able to be there for Amy when he was not able.

Bob was making a common yet tragic mistake. He was showing his love for his family by providing for them instead of spending time with them. Yet, when we genuinely love people, we spend time with them. If we really love our children, we will spend time with them. Bob has reset his priorities and is coming home earlier now. It may cost him a promotion, but that is a risk he is willing to take. God will take care of him.

Lord, help us to set our time aside to love what is really important.

Consider the work of God;
For who can make straight what
He has made crooked?
—ECCL. 7:13

Have you ever taken a wire clothes hanger and bent it at about a forty-five-degree angle and then tried to straighten it out to its original form? It is impossible to do, no matter what tools you use. The same can be said of bent auto frames or folded writing paper. We can add one other item to the list: the universe. Many people try desperately to get others to live in harmony. Others have taken on an equally formidable task: straightening out their own bent lives. Both tasks are impossible.

Solomon learned that he did not have the power to change either himself or the world to the point of perfection. His comment, today's verse, was not meant to be pessimistic. He is not presenting God as one who arbitrarily decided he would make this a corrupt world. He is communicating the world of reality as it is. We can only produce lasting change when we understand our limitations in life. Do not be abhorred when you do not see your life progressing smoothly. God fully understands your limitations in the context of a bent existence. May this verse be an encouragement to you to rest in God, who knows his way through this maze.

Lord, help us to accept our station in life knowing that you are here.

*Husbands, love your wives, just as Christ also loved
the church and gave Himself for it.*
—EPH. 5:25

I spotted a symptom of addiction on a recent airing of
"The Cosby Show." Claire and Cliff Huxtable were discussing life with their future son-in-law. He commented
about Cliff doing a "woman's job" and Claire hit the
roof. She launched into a tirade in which she stated
that a healthy marriage was one where the partners
did their part and met each other halfway. The audience exploded with applause! She had shown that
punk!

But all she had shown was that America has been
duped by a performance-based system of acceptance
called the 50/50 relationship. The system does not
work for one simple reason: a husband's measurement
of his efforts will not match his wife's measurement of
what he did, and vice versa. He may measure his effort
in a particular area and call it 60 percent; as she saw it
he barely managed to do 30 percent.

The 50/50 system results in requiring a mate to perform on the basis of someone else's standard of acceptance, which no one can successfully do for long. Some
form of abuse usually takes place at that point.

---

*Scripture commands us to love unconditionally. How do you and your
spouse work out a successful and healthy marriage?*

> *And Jacob gave Esau bread and stew of lentils;*
> *then he ate and drank, arose, and went his way.*
> *Thus Esau despised his birthright.*
>
> —GEN. 25:34

What lovely penmanship!" the teacher exclaimed as she looked past you at Sally, who was sitting next to you. Sally beamed and you became more nervous. "Very nice," she said to you, "but it could be a little neater." What child has never battled inferiority from the comparative environment of school? The result is often a compulsive or inadequate child.

Workaholism may begin in the home but it ferments in school. The academic community is a perfect breeding ground for performance-oriented people.

I know. I lived and worked in an academic community for fifteen years, both as a student and an instructor. I have felt the pressure to perform for the *summa cum laude* at the expense of my family and even my own health. (I never did get it, by the way.) I saw my colleagues do the same. I will never forget what one professor told us, "Don't be so wrapped up in your grade. As soon as you receive your diploma no one will care." She was right. Like Esau, I wonder how many other ways we sacrifice what is really important for the incidentals.

God, help us not to sell our eternal inheritance for a mess of this temporary pottage.

For they had not understood about the loaves,
because their heart was hardened.

—MARK 6:52

The hard heart is not a description in Scripture that is used exclusively about the infidel. In this setting Mark is describing the state of Christ's disciples. How did they come to be hardened and oblivious to the work of God? Did they give in to temptation? Did they develop an addiction that ruled their lives? No. In the early part of the chapter they were commissioned to go forth and do the work of God with power and the display of miracles. They succeeded, and they came back in such an excited state that Jesus had to make them rest. Then they witnessed firsthand the feeding of the five thousand. Finally they experienced Jesus walking on the water and calming the wind for them at a word. It was in this context that our verse was uttered. What caused their hardness? Overwork. The greatest foe to a balanced life is feeling that we have to keep our noses so close to the grindstone that we miss the wonderful things around us. Overwork is one of the early signs of burnout.

Lord Jesus, touch our hearts daily and keep us soft. May we never lose sight of the wonder of your work around us as we labor.

"Like a woman forsaken and grieved in spirit,
Like a youthful wife when you were refused."
—ISA. 54:6

Another way in which our addictiveness forces us to relate in marriage deals with "Fantasy Love." When the honeymoon is over and the real work of making a marriage becomes tiresome, addicts fantasize in an effort to neutralize the pain and escape reality.

Because an addict is self-seeking and out of control, he tries to recapture the romance that existed while dating. The rationale for the search is usually "the grass is greener on the other side of the fence."

Then he develops a new relationship with either a real person or a mental image of one who can restore the lost feelings. The new relationship is just like dating: all very positive and accompanied by very little reality or responsibility. It is a fantasy that is so satisfying at this point that our mate cannot compete.

We forget that any grass on the other side of the fence eventually will need to be mowed, too. We barge ahead and reject our mate and enter another relationship without commitment.

O God, keep me from forcing my mate to compete with an illusion centered around my own pleasure-seeking.

Oh, the depth of the riches both of the wisdom and knowledge of God! How unsearchable are His judgments and His ways past finding out!
—ROM. 11:33

But do you *really* know God?" The preacher's words were cutting us like a knife. We were in chapel at a Christian college where I was a student years ago. The message he was preaching on, "Knowing God," is still with me to this day. I ask myself that question regularly and always get the same answer: "More than I used to, not as much as I need to, hopefully not less than I think."

Step Three of the Twelve Step program for recovery says, "Made a decision to turn our will and lives over to the care of God as we understood him." That is a tough one, isn't it? We are never really able to understand God fully. Our verse today was uttered by Paul, not out of frustration and despair, but in praise of God's goodness! While we will never feel adequate in our knowledge of God, we may rest assured that he has a full knowledge of us. That is all we need to trust him with our lives. Have you made that decision today? Do you rest in the conviction that God knows you better than you know yourself? It is a liberating experience.

When you cannot see God's hand you can always see his heart.

> *Likewise you wives, be submissive to your own
> husbands, that even if some do not obey the word,
> they, without a word, may be won by the conduct
> of their wives.*
> —1 PETER 3:1

Kathy had said everything she could possibly say in every way it could possibly be said and all to no avail. John was immovable, resolute, stubborn, and unresponsive about her concerns. He was gone so much that the children did not even notice his presence or absence anymore, and even when he was home he was always at his computer working on something.

Nothing worked until she quit. The key was that she simultaneously quit on *two* fronts. He immediately detected the obvious way she quit. No longer did she nag. Oh, she still revealed her feelings in the form of "I" statements, but no more nagging and encouraging.

The second way she quit was invisible but powerful. She quit carrying his responsibilities. She went about her business of caring for herself and the children as best she could, and he could not stand it.

When she backed off, he looked up. According to the verse, it works that way.

Are you willing to give that a try in your marriage? Do you have anything to lose, or is something working better?

*Therefore I take pleasure in infirmities, in
reproaches, in needs, in persecutions, in distresses,
for Christ's sake. For when I am weak,
then I am strong.* —2 COR. 12:10

Phil was trying to understand the concept of "letting
go." He remembered that often as a child his father
drilled into him the importance of winning. Sometimes
when Phil made a mistake his father criticized him in
front of others. No matter how hard he tried Phil could
never please his father. Phil's whole life was built on
striving to be a success, but unconsciously he was angry at his father for his unrealistic expectations.

Phil approached counseling with the same success
orientation that he used at work. Unconsciously he
wanted to be the perfect counselee and zip straight
through the recovery steps. Week after week he expected himself to make progress.

For a homework assignment I instructed him to play
a game with his daughter and plan on making three
big mistakes on purpose. The following week he was
very dejected because he had failed to fail. This
quickly turned to joy when he realized that he had
"failed" and survived.

Lord, thank you for giving me the freedom to just do my best.

"Or how can you say to your brother, 'Brother, let me remove the speck that is in your eye,' when you yourself do not see the plank that is in your own eye? Hypocrite! First remove the plank from your own eye, and then you will see clearly to remove the speck that is in your brother's eye."

—LUKE 6:42

What is your family motto?" I asked the group. It is a provocative way to help people think about their families of origin. Some responses I hear are quite popular, like "Do your best" or "We will support whatever you do." These are healthy mottoes, but others are not so healthy. One man shared his motto that was like the motto of many. "Don't do as I do, do as I say." In some homes this motto is not admitted to; in others it is quite explicit. The parents wish to keep their children from making the same mistakes they did. They justify the motto as an act of love. The result, however, is confusion in the children's minds and the breakdown of discipline. The adult child will spend years trying to determine the proper attitudes and actions that should have been determined in youth.

Do not allow yourself to fall into the same trap. Think about the double messages you may be sending to your children.

Remember the old saying, "Practice what you preach."

> *"So I sought for a man among them who would
> make a wall, and stand in the gap before Me on
> behalf of the land, that I should not destroy it; but I
> found no one."* —EZEK. 22:30

A workaholic or a perfectionist is just one of the crowd. You may object to that and point out that the workaholic is doing more than anyone else, or that the perfectionist is doing something better than anyone else. But you're still merely comparing with the rest of the crowd and being best of a group. That is still being just one of the group.

God's intention is that we be truly unique and stand out from the crowd. He is looking for individuals, not people-pleasers. Here in Ezekiel he says he is searching for *a single person* to stand for him against the oppression taking place in the land.

It must have been as frightening then to stand out from the crowd as it is today, for in Ezekiel he "found no one." But he did not always come up empty. Look at Hebrews chapter 11. It is often called the "Hall of Faith" and is a long list of those who refused to just be one of the crowd; they rejected the position of being the healthiest of a group of sick people.

And you? If God could protect and empower those in Hebrews 11, does it seem that he could do so again? Volunteer to him today.

Then He arose and rebuked the wind, and said to
the sea, "Peace, be still!" And the wind ceased
and there was a great calm. —MARK 4:39

A mouse in a maze" was the way Jean described her upbringing. She was alluding to the sense of confusion a mouse experiences as it struggles to find the cheese at the end of the maze. Jean saw herself as that mouse with one difference: her parents never placed the cheese at the end of her task. Not only was there no reward, she had only criticism to prod her on. She was reared in a home where both parents were high achievers who demanded perfection from their children. A mother of three, Jean was in therapy at our clinic after spending time in a hospital for acute anxiety and depression. Her emotions were like a runaway train that had built up tremendous momentum.

Today Jean is learning to relax even though a little voice still screams at her to get moving. She is practicing how to rebel against the "ought's" and obey her God of grace.

Jesus is able to speak and command calmness of the sea; likewise he is able to command calmness in our souls. The key to calmness is to obey Jesus and be still.

May God's grace overpower our grimace.

*Then he said to them, "You know how unlawful it
is for a Jewish man to keep company with or go to
one of another nation. But God has shown me that
I should not call any man common or unclean."*
—ACTS 10:28

Barry's attitudes helped to perpetuate his physical illness. Virtually anyone who was not identical to him in
his lineage, shade of skin, and cultural background was
undesirable in his book. I've never seen a more cynical
and bitter man.

He never participated in counseling. He had his pre-
conceived set of answers and was not interested in en-
tertaining any questions that might make him
reconsider his position.

Barry's resentment has taken a heavy toll on him
and his health. At last word he was requiring more
surgery.

The Scripture provides an opportunity to leave our
ingrained prejudices without the need to rationalize or
prove the merits of changing our stance. Peter, Jewish
to the core, heard from God that no man was unholy or
unclean by virtue of his nationality.

*Step Eight necessitates making amends to people we have hurt.
Whether it is based in ethnic pride or not, is there anyone you have
been prejudiced against to whom you need to apologize for your own
health?*

> *And let us not grow weary while doing good, for in*
> *due season we shall reap if we do not lose heart.*
> —GAL. 6:9

I was sitting in rush-hour traffic one evening and looked over at the car next to me. The driver leaned against the window ledge, his forehead in his hand, and pushed his hair up. He looked stressed and tired after a long day's work. I thought about how tired I felt and it dawned on me that everyone is tired most of the time.

When we're tired our nerves are on edge and it only takes a small spark to set off an explosion. How soothing it is to hear a kind word from another that will turn that fatigue into serenity. We can't avoid the traffic jams and the stress, but we certainly can make it easier for each other. We, who know the Lord, realize there is a special advantage to helping those who are making this journey with us.

When we overextend ourselves we tend to focus on our own issues and forget that there are others wrestling with the same issues. Being too tired can cause us to miss out on important matters of life.

Lord, help us to find the rest we need to help others.

Come and see the works of God;
He is awesome in His doing toward
the sons of men. —PS. 66:5

I learned a valuable lesson many years ago while I was in the middle of a job transition. I was fortunate enough to have several weeks off, which I hoped to use for some much-needed rest. So I took a backpacking trip using the shelters along the eighty-mile Laurel Ridge Trail.

I planned each day to go eight to ten miles and then do absolutely nothing. I discovered that "nothing" was not easy for someone used to being so responsible at work. Each day I found myself pushing to get to my next destination. I was organized enough to weather a hurricane, forest fire, or Armageddon! What I didn't plan was an all-day downpour on the third day.

By midday I reached the first of the shelter areas and decided to rest and dry out before the second half of my journey. I built a fire and took a nap only to wake up to find a burning hole on the side of my boot. Two days earlier I would have been livid with myself for this self-administered hot-foot, but instead I broke into a giant laugh. I still have those boots as a memorial to walk a lot slower in life and not work so hard.

Do you push too hard in your leisure and treat it like work? Plan to spend some time slowly enjoying some part of God's creation.

> *So God created man in His own image; in the*
> *image of God He created him; male and female*
> *He created them.*
> —GEN. 1:27

Who am I" is a question the philosophers have wrestled with for centuries. When the Shah of Iran was deposed, his family left their homeland, wealth, and power and have only the memories of what they were. We are a bit like that.

We are created in the image of God. We were created perfect and were made to reign with God. However, we were dethroned, if you will, by sin. We now walk around with a figment of that image of God in us, clouded by the sin that distorts everything it comes in contact with. We have an inkling of what we were created to be but have no way of attaining it.

That is why we become so frustrated with ourselves. We expect far more from ourselves than is possible. We have never accepted imperfection as a part of life, and we never will. But God has accepted us in spite of our shortcomings and is doing something about it. He is conforming us back into his image through our walk with Christ.

The key to life is to accept our plight as reality and realize that it is God's good determination to restore that image. He asks only that we trust him to do his perfect work.

Let us abandon our demands in life and let God be God.

When Christ who is our life appears, then you also will appear with Him in glory.   —COL. 3:4

Mark had looked in many places but had settled on what he thought was the answer to his problems: homosexuality. It promised to meet his needs for acceptance, pleasure, and significance. He thought it was real life and could not at first see the death in it.

Mark was a Christian with a great deal of abuse in his background. While searching for emotional pain relievers, he had stumbled into the homosexual world. He had had enough reservations not to become a participating member immediately. He attributes that to the protection of God.

He came for counseling because of his conflicting emotions. Homosexual friends promised him all he wanted to hear, but it sounded too good to him. He questioned whether *anything* could give the complete satisfaction they said he could find if he would just commit.

Mark worked hard in therapy. He broke through much of the pain of his past when he grasped a phrase in today's verse: "Christ who is our life."

When Mark reminded himself that Christ was his life the inner turmoil began to subside. Do you have conflicts that need quieting?

Your ears shall hear a word behind you, saying,
"This is the way, walk in it."   —ISA. 30:21

I heard a quip recently from a former attorney. He said that lawyers practice law until they figure out what they really want to do with their lives. It reminded me of Joe, who had come to counseling for depression. He was a lawyer who hated his work. To him it was boring and certainly not glamorous. He only became an attorney because his parents wanted him to be one and because it was prestigious. He felt empty, hollow, and trapped.

He wasn't lazy and unmotivated as you might think. In actuality he was driven in his work. He tried to find satisfaction from his work by achieving more. He hoped that he would gain enough financially so he would have the freedom to do something different. Joe also worked harder to suppress the pain of doing work he did not enjoy. It sounds strange, doesn't it?

Are you in Joe's position? It is easy to say, "Quit your job; go follow your heart," but we know it is not that simple. You can train for a different career and plan on a change down the road. Be creative. If you feel it is too late to change, seek counsel for it.

Life is too short to waste, too long to be miserable.

But those who wait on the Lord
Shall renew their strength;
They shall mount up with wings like eagles.
—ISA. 40:31

John and I were taking one of our students to his home deep in the African bush country. A head wind blew constantly. The dirt road followed the ridge line of the mountain range and dropped into deep valleys on either side of us. Often we had to maneuver our pickup through scattered boulders that littered the mountaintop.

I was driving, and John was first to see the eagle. He was flying into the wind, the same direction as we were driving. He was not more than twenty yards from us and was a sight to behold. None of us had ever seen such a bird in flight from so short a distance before.

We had traveled beside the eagle for more than five minutes before we realized that he had not once flapped his wings. He merely had them fully extended and was literally riding on the wind. He was not working; he was using the power of the wind.

God has never intended that we become superstrong in order to live the Christian life. His plan has always been for us to ride on his wind.

Have you been riding the wind or beating your wings?

> *For what will it profit a man if he gains the whole world, and loses his own soul?* —MARK 8:36

Mary worked for a branch of the government that was short-staffed and overworked. She had been with the department for close to twenty years and had gained the reputation of a reliable and thorough team member who could be counted on. Her supervisor knew that and appreciated her for it—and that was the problem. Her boss was a workaholic who volunteered for many projects but then delegated the responsibilities to his staff. Mary's job description became a joke; her responsibilities far outweighed that job definition. She didn't mind the work, but she didn't want to make it her life. Her home was a mess and her marriage was strained. Mary was suffering from vicarious workaholism.

Vicarious workaholism is a contagious disease. The only cure for it seems more painful than the disease itself. The key is to draw boundaries for the boss when he will not draw them for you. You must learn to say no. You must be willing to quit your job if necessary. God intends for us to be good employees, but not at all costs.

———————————

Don't be held hostage by the words "If you don't do it, we'll find someone who will."

And you, fathers, do not provoke your children to wrath, but bring them up in the training and admonition of the Lord.
—EPH. 6:4

Bill was looking forward to a weekend with his family. They had complained recently about his frequently being late and working overtime.

He was home that Friday just in time to greet his ten-year-old son, Mike. Mike came bursting in and said, "Hey, Dad, can we toss the football?" Bill said, "Sure, but first tell me about your day." "Well, I did get an A on a book report I did. What do you think of that?"

As Mike waited for a response from his father he didn't know the word *report* had triggered another thought in Bill. "Report? Report! Oh, no! I forgot to finish the monthly sales report!"

Mike continued to wait and finally said, "Hey, Dad, are you zoned out?" Bill snapped out of his panic, smiled at Mike, and told him to go get the football. He realized that he had a few more miles to go before he would have a handle on his workaholism.

Father, forgive me for all those times I have made promises I never kept. Help me to pay attention and realize when I'm being controlled by work.

> *"Is this not the carpenter. . . ."* And suddenly a voice
> came from heaven, saying, *"This is My beloved Son,*
> *in whom I am well pleased."*
> —MARK 6:3; MATT. 3:17

The occasion of this passage is the baptism of Christ. Up to this point Jesus had not performed a miracle or taught a parable. He had not started his public ministry. In spite of this God says, "This is My beloved Son, in whom I am well pleased."

What had Jesus been doing all this time? He was being faithful. For years, in an obscure village Jesus had labored as a carpenter. The remarkable thing is that this event took place when Jesus was nearly thirty years old; his ministry lasted only three years!

Sometimes we become impatient with ourselves when we do not see the progress in our lives that we demand. As a therapist I continually exhort my clients to accept the fact that growth is a slow, arduous process. I also must remember to remind myself of the same. Let's remember that our sons and daughters need the same reprieve from us.

Lord, help us to see ourselves as you see us; help us to rejoice in our faithfulness more than our successes. And above all, help us to accept our failures.

Be diligent to know the state of your flocks,
And attend to your herds.

—PROV. 27:23

Since I had never authored anything beyond a paper for graduate school, writing these devotionals was a unique experience. The idea of deadlines was not new, but the volume of output in the time allowed made for a great increase in my stress index.

The extra pressure showed up in my family. My wife, shouldering more of the load, tired more easily. Our three boys seemed to increase their clamor for time with Dad, but in retrospect they were just asking for their normal share of my time, which was going into this writing project instead.

Projects do that to those of us with "isms" like workaholism and perfectionism. And projects have a way of stacking up like books. We tell ourselves and our families that they need to bear with us just till this thing is done. But as soon as one project is completed there is usually another demanding the same amount of attention.

For a while now, my middle name has been No. I need to take control again and stop grinding from one project to the next. I need to heed the principles about which I have just written. How about you?

December 11 – AVOIDING AVOIDANCE

And I said, "Should such a man as I flee?"
—NEH. 6:11

I used to be a workaholic," Joe confided to me. I knew he had recovered because his life was a model of balance. "How did you gain control of it?" I asked. He went on to tell me how he had burned out, lost a multimillion dollar business he had started, and came to know Jesus Christ. But the main issue that caused the overwork in the first place was old fashioned avoidance. He said he hated to go home and stayed at the office to avoid his wife. She had been overly dependent on him to keep her going emotionally. When they first met, her dependence made him feel important. But after they were married he had come to the end of his resources to satisfy her. So he escaped. Things went from bad to worse and they eventually divorced.

This is a cold, cruel world we live in, and the one true refuge we have is our homes. Joe found that all the money he made did not replace the pain of alienation. By the grace of God he has rebuilt his life, started a new home, and is living in balance. At fifty years old he has a new lease on life simply because he determined to do something about it. If you are having family problems do not avoid them. Seek help.

Lord, help us to stand fast in the battle and not flee.

*Therefore we must give the more earnest heed to
the things we have heard, lest we drift away.*
—HEB. 2:1

A good way to maintain boundaries is to give yourself new permission to take care of yourself. We need to say to ourselves, "I am entitled to be myself," and live a balanced lifestyle free of having to perform during every waking hour.

On the surface this may sound selfish but it is a prerequisite to responsible behavior that is not driven by compulsion.

Think of your inner self like a work organization. In order for new work to begin, it first must be authorized. The new work must be permitted before the action phase begins.

Our God has created us with needs. He intends for us to meet those needs in responsible ways according to his will.

_____

*Lord, help me believe that I long ago had your permission to exist
and can now echo this approval myself.*

*For we dare not . . . compare ourselves with those
who commend themselves. But they, measuring
themselves by themselves, and comparing
themselves among themselves, are not wise.*
—2 COR. 10:12

Judy was gaining weight, and she noticed that her strength was not what it used to be. Her awareness of her mortality was made even more acute when she would see younger, bikini-clad women on TV. She began to overlook the trade-off that comes with age: the stability of her marriage, her spiritual maturity, her accrued wisdom and knowledge.

Judy exhibits a danger every person must guard against: the innate tendency to compare ourselves with others. We cannot help this tendency, but we can challenge it when it comes to mind. The apostle Paul said that we are not wise when we allow ourselves to fall into that trap. We will go to one of two extremes: Either we will compare our weaknesses against another's strengths and feel inferior or we will deny our weaknesses and downplay the strength of others. God wants us to look to him for the standard of measurement; only he has a clear picture of where we are going.

---

*Lord, help us to resist the temptation to compare ourselves with
others without consulting you first.*

*Let your speech always be with grace, seasoned
with salt, that you may know how you ought to
answer each one.*   —COL. 4:6

Step Nine was probably the most difficult for Alice. It
required that she make amends to those whom she had
offended and injured. Her perfectionism had developed in her a caustic and acidic way of speaking to
most everyone. It was such a habit that even when
she prayed there was sarcasm evident to her in how
she talked to God.

Alice had to first become reconciled to herself. She
had to challenge the self-talk that was demeaning and
hurtful to her. With practice she began to come to
terms with herself and stopped beating herself up.

Next she began to make amends to the other people
in her life. There were a few she had to contact directly. She spoke to her family face-to-face. That was
the most difficult but also the most liberating. Others
she phoned, still others she wrote. She had to replace
her cutting way of relating with a different way of communicating, using grace and compassion instead.

*How much of your communication needs to be seasoned with grace
and compassion instead of demands? Try asking those closest to you.*

He has made everything beautiful in its time.
—ECCL. 3:11

We all remember the childhood story "The Ugly Duckling," about an ugly little bird that grew up with the ducks and was mocked and scorned because it was so homely and different. As it grew, it developed into a beautiful swan, thereby gaining the respect of the other birds. The moral of the story, so we tell our children, is that we should not judge the circumstances based on the perceptions that we hold at the time. What starts out as ugly may in fact become beautiful. What may seem tragic may later be viewed as a blessing in disguise.

This verse offers a phenomenal insight into God's role in the affairs of our lives. He is keenly aware of our pain and suffering. I love to hear someone reflect on the hardships of her life and say that she wouldn't trade the experience for anything. God is so much in control of your destiny that he can truly make everything beautiful in his own time. If you believe him it will help heal the pain and anger of past offenses more rapidly than you can imagine.

Lord, help us to trust that you are in control.

You come short in no gift, eagerly waiting for the revelation of our Lord Jesus Christ.
—1 COR. 1:7

As Christmas approached our youngest son couldn't wait to open the gifts under the tree. We knew that on Christmas Eve we could expect the traditional campaign for opening one of the gifts early. The difficult part for children is the long wait. Yet in spite of this strong surge of emotional energy they wait in faith and modify their behavior so as not to be seen unfavorable by the gift giver.

After a year of recovery we too await Christmas. We have asked for grace in those relationships that have suffered because of our overwork. We have also asked for the capacity to get in touch with our feelings and to face our fears.

The good news of Christmas is that God has heard these prayer requests and has a few surprises waiting for us. If we can wait in faith, eagerly anticipating this future time, we will be filled with joy when it happens. We will also learn self-discipline along the way because the victory has been purchased by Christ.

God, as your child in faith I eagerly anticipate your gifts to me.

> *Beloved, I beg you as sojourners and pilgrims,*
> *abstain from fleshly lusts, which war against the*
> *soul.*
> 1 PETER 2:11

Lewis had been seduced again. Not by a woman, but by his workaholism. He had come to grips with its existence in his life and had sincerely worked at ending it. But he had slipped again last week and was disappointed with himself. He thought his previous work had been wasted.

Step Ten indicates that even though we may be well aware of the deadly and painful consequences of following our addictions, the "ism" itself has a seductive element to it. The only way for Lewis to deal with this aspect of his recovery was to monitor his old tendencies regularly and continually.

The message today is that our human needs are a bottomless pit that can never be filled by earthly ingredients. The implication is that the antidote is spiritual.

Lord Christ, help me to continue to look to you to have needs met. Help me to recognize when I unintentionally try to meet those needs with a false substitute.

*Confess your trespasses to one another, and pray
for one another.*   —JAMES 5:16

I recently saw a little boy of five or six fall and hurt his
knee while playing. He stood up and grimaced, obviously wanting to cry, but choked back his tears. He
hurriedly jumped back into the game to cover his em-
barrassment.

Our society values stoicism. It has always encouraged the repression of emotions, particularly anger
and pain. As an adult, the overachiever, workaholic
carries out these commands to perfection: never admit
fault, never take responsibility, never show pain or
hurt. Never let them see you sweat, as athletes, come-
dians, and businessmen expound on the deodorant
television commercials. It is seen as a sign of weakness.

What a contrast the commands of Scripture: confess
your faults, admit your weaknesses, reconcile with
others, practice humility. These are fundamental principles that God has designed to give us reprieve from
the stress and anger of life. We must keep in touch with
God's contrasting perspectives, remembering that we
do not have to carry the burden of what others think of
us. It will certainly lighten your load!

Humble yourself and let God exalt you.

> *"Judge not, and you shall not be judged. Condemn not, and you shall not be condemned. Forgive, and you will be forgiven. Give, and it will be given to you."*
>
> —LUKE 6:37–38

It was an exceptionally busy day at the clinic and, as often occurs toward the end of the day, my desk looked like Mt. St. Helens. Scheduling had been extremely difficult for my new patient Fred, who had canceled three times at the last minute due to work conflicts.

I had run late, and Fred seemed irritated when I apologized for my tardiness. Going through his social history seemed like pulling teeth. Fred said the appointment was his wife's idea but that she had the problem. The more I asked him to elaborate the more displeased he seemed.

When I asked him if anything else was bothering him he said, "How on earth can you do your job with a desk that looks like that?" He proceeded to ventilate angrily how confused he was that guys with desks like mine were getting all the promotions while he did all the hard work.

Fred didn't recognize his work addiction. He was still in denial and projected blame for his problems onto others. Recovery begins when we admit to our problem and ask for help.

Consider how often you become irritated and feel unappreciated by your co-workers or employer.

Test all things; hold fast what is good.
—1 THESS. 5:21

As a resident in the Washington, D.C., area I have become sensitized to the need for control we humans cherish by the loss of control we experience in our traffic system. It is common to find commuters who spend two to three hours per day traveling to and from work, and that does not include traffic jams on the infamous Beltway. I witnessed one traffic jam that was thirteen miles long! For us urban dwellers the challenge to maintain a sense of autonomy is enormous.

We actually have very little control over what is going to happen next. Entering the cloverleaf onto the highway can be the fast way home or the "road from hell"; we never know until we make the choice, and then it is too late to turn back. The only control that anyone has over such circumstances is in the attitude that we choose to maintain during the time of trouble. The time can be well spent in meditation, listening to music, or even dreaming. Don't weave in and out of traffic and get overworked. The yardage gained is not worth the effort spent. Go prepared.

Hope for the best, expect the worst, and take what comes.

*"Blessed are the peacemakers,
For they shall be called sons of God."*
—MATT. 5:9

Susan was a perfectionist at her housework, and the Christmas season was tailor-made for enabling her compulsion. She prided herself in how meticulous she was with her holiday decorating and was frequently the envy of her peers. This year would be different, however. Susan was now in therapy working on this and other compulsive work tendencies.

In years past, her husband and children dreaded the holidays because of her behavior. The house had to be perfect and the children always had to be dressed immaculately. Her husband, Tom, had to do the mechanical work that Susan couldn't do.

In family counseling Susan learned the roots of her perfectionism. This year she let the whole family participate in decisions about decorating. She learned to laugh when her family teased her about being a perfectionist. She also laughed on Christmas morning, when the family discovered all her gifts wrapped in newspaper. To her this was a symbol of letting go.

This holiday season, look back at your traditions and see to what extent you have allowed others to freely add their own ideas. Ask the Lord to help you establish traditions at Christmas that provide joy for all.

Blessed is the man
Who walks not in the counsel of the ungodly,
Nor stands in the path of sinners,
Nor sits in the seat of the scornful;
But his delight is in the law of the Lord,
And in His law he meditates day and night.
He shall be like a tree
Planted by the rivers of water,
That brings forth its fruit in its season,
Whose leaf also shall not wither;
And whatever he does shall prosper.

—PS. 1:1–3

The process of maintaining a recovery from workaholism or perfectionism is continual. The subtle and seductive nature of these addictions makes steady maintenance all the more necessary. Ultimately, we need to renew our belief systems. That comes only as we replace false tapes that play in our minds with what is real and true.

Meditating on Scripture is like a cow chewing its cud. It will chew on it a while, then chew on it again later. This portion of Psalm 1 is an excellent place to start.

Begin to memorize it today.

> *You stiff-necked and uncircumcised in heart and*
> *ears! You always resist the Holy Spirit; as your*
> *fathers did, so do you.*   —ACTS 7:51

One of my daughters was having a difficult time recently. She was angry and was showing it in both tongue and posture. I remember sitting at the table and reaching behind her head to draw her near. I felt her neck stiffen as she drew back. She would have no part of it at this moment. Her resistance was great.

The word *stiff-necked* is an obscure word, but one that does not require a definition. The speaker of this verse was Stephen, who moments later would be stoned to death for speaking the truth of God. He was calling the Jews stiff-necked because they were resisting God and following the useless traditions that kept them in bondage. The workaholic is much like that. Many people loathe their captivity to perfectionism but refuse to consider other options. Like my daughter they pull back at the slightest suggestion to relax, delegate, or say no.

Loosen up. Do not resist what is best for you.

If the Son therefore shall make you free, ye shall be free indeed.

*And the things that you have heard from me among
many witnesses, commit these to faithful men who
will be able to teach others also.* —2 TIM. 2:2

Educators tell us this all the time, that the best way to
learn anything is to teach it to others. The principle is
especially true regarding recovery from an addiction
to workaholism, perfectionism, and obsessions. The
teaching of others is the cement that holds the recovery process in place.

It is more than just a principle of education. Paul
wrote the same thing to his young protégé Timothy
way back in the first century. Communism recognizes
the same principle and thus requires new party members to actively disciple newer recruits so that the lessons and principles become firmly embedded.

Overcoming and staying victorious over workaholism and its related diseases is the same. The best way
for the student to learn the lesson is to become a
teacher.

Is there anyone in your life you need to teach? You have been a student. Can you see yourself as a teacher? It is called full-circle recovery. You can do it.

> *[I am] confident of this very thing, that He who has*
> *begun a good work in you will complete it until the*
> *day of Jesus Christ.*
> —PHIL. 1:6

Debbie's perfectionism and obsession with her weight had consumed her life and driven her family crazy. But finally she had begun to deal with the roots of addiction instead of focusing on only the weight symptom. She had made great progress, and her perfectionism was much more subdued.

Then she came for our appointment one day looking defeated. She had slipped. In the last week she had tried two new diets, and she had been upset with one of her children who made only an A- in one of his college courses. She said, "But I had dealt with all that stuff! Why is it back?"

Debbie had made the common mistake of thinking that because she had recognized a problem and made great progress in overcoming it, it was gone forever. She did not understand the automatic nature of her illness. Even though she had uncovered the addiction as the enemy, she would still tend to follow those inclinations.

The difference was that now she could recognize the perfectionism and stop it in its early stages, before it developed any momentum.

The Scripture promises a process of recovery, that the Lord began the
good work of correcting us and he will continue to perfect his work.

> *"Only take heed to yourself, and diligently keep yourself, lest you forget the things your eyes have seen, lest they depart from your heart all the days of your life. And teach them to your children and your grandchildren."*
> —DEUT. 4:9

It took less than a year and he was gone. He was the picture of health at thirty-nine. He regularly jogged and exercised and was known as a disciplined man.

He had been the bright and shining star in a city and a career filled with many bright lights. He had engineered the election of a president and was subsequently named to be the head of his political party. He had rewritten how to run a campaign, and done it before reaching forty. And then, at forty, he died from an inoperable brain tumor.

In his last year, two items seemed to dominate his thinking. He publicly spoke of his children, how he would miss them and how he desired to spend as much of the remainder of his life as was possible with them. He also apologized to many former political "enemies."

A man does not usually spend much time with his family when he is overseeing the election of the next president. But the certainty of death changes a person's priorities.

———————

Lee Atwater knew when his life would end. You and I may not know how many days we have left, but could it be possible that we need to reprioritize our lives as he did and mend some relationships and focus on our children more than we are doing now?

> *Be anxious for nothing, but in everything by prayer*
> *and supplication, with thanksgiving, let your*
> *requests be made known to God; and the peace of*
> *God, which surpasses all understanding, will guard*
> *your hearts and your minds through Christ Jesus.*
> —PHIL. 4:6–7

Fear has a consistent way of renumbering our priorities.

As I recall the news report indicated there were four of them, all reporters. They were covering the war in the Persian Gulf and had ventured either into or simply too close to the Iraqi border, when they were taken prisoner. They were tortured and threatened and seriously doubted that they would be allowed to live.

But they survived and were released.

In the televised news report of their ordeal, they revealed how they had responded to the fear of dying they experienced. One man in particular spoke of his planning to spend more time with his wife and children if he were ever set free. He attributed this to how facing death had helped him see what was truly important in life.

_____

The command in today's verse not to be anxious implies that anxiety is automatic when we're afraid. I have not been captured and threatened with death from an enemy, but I have my own fears. I need to ask myself if I am "using" those fears to give my family priority in my life.

*"No longer do I call you servants, for a servant
does not know what his master is doing; but I have
called you friends, for all things that I heard from
My Father I have made known to you."*
—JOHN 15:15

Jeannie, Sue, and Donna have a great deal in common, even though they have never met. They are all perfectionists, driven to excel, successful career women, and overly dependent on men. And they all grew up receiving double messages from one or both parents.

Double messages are frequently expressed in terms of "Do as I say, not as I do." Each of these women was given the role of "the last great hope": They were told, in essence, "I want you to live your own life and follow your desires./You have been my salvation, I can't make it through this trouble without you." The emotional result in each of these women was an overdeveloped sense of responsibility and dependence on others. They were never given "permission" to think for themselves. They lived in a world of confusing rules, where they had to learn to read between the lines.

How good it is to realize that God has no hidden messages. He does not say that he loves us unconditionally and then threaten to abandon us if we fail him. Nor does he *need* us for his emotional survival. That frees us to depend on him. And we can relax in that!

Stop reading between the lines. Adult: I will stop reading between the lines when you stop putting so much there!

The secret things belong to the LORD our God, but those things which are revealed belong to us and to our children forever, that we may do all the words of this law.
—DEUT. 29:29

We all have our favorite movies and stories. One of mine is the Indiana Jones adventure *Raiders of the Lost Ark*. The hero, Jones, was in search of a missing jewel that, once affixed to a pole, would reflect the sun's rays and reveal the place of the long lost biblical Ark of the Covenant. He had all the information he needed to find the Ark, but until he put the missing jewel in its proper place, all his information was of little use.

In our work with many religious people, we have come to realize that they share a similar problem with Indy Jones. They seem to possess all of the information needed to live a moral and productive life, yet lack the jewel that will help them relax. Most driven, perfectionistic people lack this quality as well. They will continue digging in the wrong place until they can acquire that jewel that will bring them the rest and enjoyment for their efforts.

The missing jewel is the gem of *grace*. Grace is defined as getting what we do not deserve. God has based the entire New Testament on this concept and we can only understand true peace and find rest as we accept grace for ourselves. It is the primary remedy for perfectionism.

_____

God has hidden the Ark of the Covenant; He has revealed grace plainly to us!

"But many who are first will be last, and the last first."
—MATT. 19:30

One of the basic concepts of Christianity that is often overlooked or misunderstood is that of *paradox*. Webster's defines a paradox as "a statement that is seemingly contradictory or opposed to common sense and yet is perhaps true."

The paradoxical concepts used to communicate truth in Scripture are numerous: "For whosoever exalteth himself shall be abased; and he that humbleth himself shall be exalted" (Luke 14:11). "He that findeth his life shall lose it: and he that loseth his life for my sake shall find it" (Matt. 10:39).

We must train our minds to look beyond our feelings and common sense to analyze correctly the paradoxes in our lives. What we often interpret as a "bad" circumstance, God may be working as good. We usually do not see it at the time, but with the discipline of analyzing what is happening, we can try to see from God's perspective and broaden our understanding. And our faith.

You see, it takes faith to go against our common sense, to do what is not natural for us. At the time we most doubt God's involvement we should focus our praise on him.

Learn to respond and not react; it will transform your relationships and your walk through life.

There is a fine line between faith and foolishness.

*"Daniel, servant of the living God, has your God,
whom you serve continually, been able to deliver
you from the lions?"*
—DAN. 6:20

You are either a Lion or a Christian. Such is the philosophy of the supervisor of a client of mine who works for one of the "big eight" accounting firms. The burnout rate was incredible.

Donna came to see me because of her inability to cope with the stress of the corporation's constant expectations of employees to sell their souls to the company store. It was also the time of the year for the annual "Lions vs. Christians" meeting of the supervisors. The purpose of the meeting was to weed out the employees who had not met the expectations of the company, sacrifice them by layoff, and then distribute their benefits among the Lions.

Donna survived but has decided to take her Certified Public Accounting credentials and enter a different field entirely. It is a risk for her. She will have to backtrack and go to school again. Her commitment to doing right—to living a healthy life—will carry her through.

Our verse for today has a parallel unknown to the corporation. As Daniel the prophet was cast in with the lions, he was protected from all harm. You may not be able to avoid being cast in with the lions if you do what is best. But you will be in good company. And you will ultimately be protected.

Lord, may we experience the same comfort you provided Daniel and Donna in the lions' den.

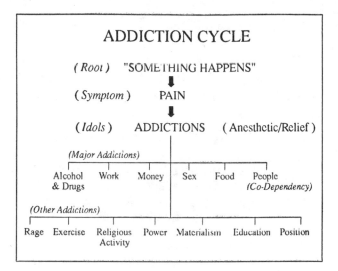

About the Authors

Gary E. Hurst specializes in marriage and family counseling at the Minirth-Meier & Byrd Clinic in Fairfax, Virginia. Gary is a licensed clinical social worker and serves on the National Board of Children's Ministries. He worked for seven years at a family service agency in Pittsburgh and as a field instructor for the University of Pittsburgh School of Social Work. He also has extensive experience in the clinical treatment of adolescents and their families both in residential and outpatient treatment programs. He has a B.A. in sociology and psychology from the University of Pittsburgh and a Master's in social work from the University of Connecticut.

Gary lives with his wife, Deanie, and two sons in Fairfax.

Mike Kachura is a licensed professional counselor with the Minirth-Meier & Byrd Clinic. He holds a Master of Arts in Counseling from Liberty University and is an ordained Baptist minister. Kachura served as associate director of the counseling center at Thomas Road Baptist Church in Lynchburg, Virginia, where he was also associate pastor. He was assistant professor of the Liberty University School of Lifelong Learning and instructor of counseling at Liberty University.

Mike lives with his wife, Shelly, and their three daughters in northern Virginia.

Larry D. Sides counsels married couples and individuals at the Minirth-Meier & Byrd Clinic. He is director of seminar development with Christian Family Life in Chantilly, Virginia, and assisted in the development of a counseling system for a residential program for adolescent boys. Formerly on the staff of Campus Crusade for Christ for nine years, Larry spent three of those years working in southern Africa. He received his Masters of Education in Guidance and Counseling from George Mason University.

An ordained minister, Larry lives in Fairfax with his wife, Norma, and their three boys.